PACKAGE YOUR GENIUS

5 STEPS TO BUILD YOUR MOST POWERFUL PERSONAL BRAND

AMANDA MILLER LITTLEJOHN

Copyright © 2018 Amanda Miller Littlejohn

All Rights Reserved.

No part of this book may be reproduced or utilized in any form or by any means, electronic or mechanical, including photocopying, recording, or by any information storage and retrieval system, without permission in writing from the author.

ISBN-13: 978-1985612785

ISBN-10: 198561278X

DEDICATION

For Wayne Earl Miller, the original genius. You sparked my ongoing quest to make brilliant minds visible, and were the first inspiration for my life's work.

Thank you.

AMANDA MILLER LITTLEJOHN

CONTENTS

Acknowledgments 7

Preface 8

Introduction 12

STEP 1 Get Clear on Your Brand 17

1. Face Your Genius: Reconnect with Your Childhood Self 20

2. Clarify Your Genius: Identify Your Strengths, Skills and Value 23

3. Communicate Your Genius: Package a Brand Message that Connects 34

STEP 2 Make the Case 41

4. Receipts: Show Evidence of Your Work and Value 43

5. Let Others Talk: Secure Invaluable Social Proof 57

STEP 3 Define Your Big Ideas 62

6. What to Share: Uncover Your Thought Leadership 66

7. How to Share: Develop a Personal Content Strategy 81

8. Idea to Income: Monetize Through Brand Signatures 93

9	Pivot: Reroute Your Path When the Time Comes	110

STEP 4 Make Yourself Visible — 117

10	Tap Into Social Media: Leverage Online Tools and Your Digital Presence	119
11	Package Your Ideas for the Media	129
12	Package Your Message for Public Speaking	143
13	Who Knows You: Be Intentional About Your Network	153

STEP 5 Sell Yourself — 161

14	Be Proactive - Intentionally Develop Your Opportunities	165
15	Master Your Time: Train Yourself to Be Productive	181
16	Tell a True Story: On Underselling Yourself, Imposter Syndrome	189
	Afterword	197
	Recommended Reading and Resources	205
	About the Author	206

ACKNOWLEDGMENTS

I'd like to acknowledge my family for giving me the foundation of love and support from which to pursue my passions. To my son Connor, thank you for inspiring me through your personal example of consistency and creative discipline. You made my path clear and sparked my decision to finally get this book done. To my son Logan, thank you for your words of encouragement, high standards and spirit of wonder. You inspire me to keep sharing my ideas. To my husband Marc, thank you for being a sounding board and source of encouragement. To mother Mattie, thank you for supporting me no matter what!

To all of my personal branding clients and students in my Package Your Genius Academy Community, it is my honor to help you make yourself and your work visible. Thank you for being my collective muse.

To Crystal Nicole Davis, Amber Cabral, Meredith Moore Crosby, Xina Eiland, James Walker and Reisha Moxley - thank you for offering your accountability and support at different points during the writing process!

And finally, to my dear friend Tara Jones, thank you for pouring into me with your time, a river of encouraging words, and the priceless gift of your friendship. Your love and light in my life endures.

PREFACE

I grew up in Nashville, Tennessee - the daughter of a multi-faceted engineer. My father graduated with a degree in electrical engineering from Tennessee State University in 1970, but went on to do all types of engineering from audio, computer and communications systems engineering both full-time and on the side.

To say I grew up in a house of gadgets would be an understatement. Think Sza's *Control* album cover. An exaggeration for sure, but that was kind of what life felt like sometimes for us.

From computer monitors in various stages of repair (or disrepair), to cables to a set of teakwood concert speakers (which I would later find out he assembled himself and used to do sound for the 1972 Rolling Stones American Tour stop in Knoxville), we were swimming in engineering stuff. Equipment. Gadgets.

And in the middle of his sea of gadgetry would sometimes sit my father, in between projects or on his way "across town" to wire sound for one of Nashville's mega churches. Or fix the computer network for one of the countless small businesses who depended on him when the cash registers at the store were no longer communicating with the network. Or to tinker in the sound booth at WFSK - the local am radio station on the campus of Fisk

University and one of my other random childhood playgrounds.

Needless to say, my dad was super smart and super talented. But at age 52, when he parted ways from his longtime employer after twenty years, he found himself in a situation his talent and intellect hadn't prepared him for.

I can remember being home for the summer after he'd become a full-time freelance engineer. We tried to put our heads together to figure out how to get his name and his talents out there. How could we connect his endless talents with the people who needed what he had to share?

That was the question I set out to answer then, and I walked away feeling as though I'd failed. Miserably.

Keep in mind, this was before social media and digital tools made marketing the domain of so many. At the time, I felt like I hadn't answered that question sufficiently. I certainly hadn't helped him get his name out there in a way that reflected his level of talent. And I watched how that inability to be seen for who he was and what he knew slowly ate away at him. In the beginning, it was a simple inability to find steady projects. As the years progressed, it was in my opinion a loss of confidence normal for anyone who finds themselves "out of the game" for too long. Later it spiraled into an enduring depression that followed him to the end of his life.

How is it that a person can be both the smartest

person you'd ever hope to meet and the smartest person you've never heard of? That conundrum dumbfounded me as I sought to help my father.

Years out of college and into my career, I began understand that I may not have been able to help my father get his name out there when he needed it. But that quest to help make those I consider brilliant beyond measure visible, became the clear calling of my professional life. Years later I would find myself being drawn to people in that exact scenario. But this time, I'd have the incredible timing of the internet and journalism experience to help me.

***

In 2007 I was laid off from my newspaper reporting job.

I was actually at home on maternity leave with my first child when I got the call that my staff writer position would be eliminated. Soon after hearing this news, I also found out my husband had lost his job.

It was right around the beginning of the Great Recession ushered in by the sub-prime mortgage crisis. We got caught up in all of that, and we were both unemployed with a newborn baby. To say we were terrified would be an understatement!

I went into survival mode. Drawing on all the skills I'd accumulated and a courage I never knew I had, I mustered the nerve to put myself out there. Repeatedly. Relentlessly. I found myself stammering through cold calls, calming my introverted nerves during networking events, and fumbling through the process to erect my first rudimentary website.

I signed up for new online tools and social networking platforms if they were free and I thought they could help me reach clients who needed my services. I tried any and everything at least once. At that time, I was doing communications which meant I was helping people with copywriting, website language, etc. Interestingly enough, that's something that I sort of do today, but in a different way.

To my delight and honestly my surprise, it worked. Within a few short months I **was** able to recover my lost wages and even triple my previous newspaper salary, meager as it was while working only part-time. I was working from home and had full control over my schedule. The freedom and autonomy was intoxicating. I had a new vision for how I could work, and honestly how I could live.

I built that business up and it evolved into more public relations, event management and social media consulting. It grew from me being a solitary writer to a full-fledged public relations person running a successful boutique consultancy. It was exciting to watch something I created grow.

But about four years in, I started feeling the urge to pivot. I kept hearing from people who needed help with their marketing and their branding and digital strategy. At the time, I was only working with organizations - I didn't have services for individuals.

While my business was designed to support organizations and teams, I continued to hear from individuals who needed help from someone like me.

I decided to pivot because at the time I was also really missing that one-on-one relationship with the client. The PR work that I was doing was a grind. I was relegated to being at my desk and on the phone a lot, but I wasn't working directly with my clients the way I craved. I felt isolated and lonely in my work.

I decided I was going to create services that really spoke to that need. So I decided to begin offering strategy sessions for individuals.

I didn't know where it would end up, but I loved the chance to connect with clients directly - it energized me. It was my joy and my honor to help people uncover their most unique and special attributes, expertise, and the surest pathway to a payday. It was the beginning of what I now call personal brand coaching.

I truly believe in these concepts as I've lived them and taught them to others. I know they will work for you, too.

This book is for you if you feel like I did when I started out - I knew I had a lot to offer, but I didn't have a way of connecting to the people who needed me.

This book is for you if you know you're great at what you do, you have great expertise, you do great work, but too few people know who you are.

This book is for you if you feel your interests and skills are all over the place, and you're having difficulty seeing and communicating a clear narrative for all you've done and the value you bring to the table.

This book is for you if you're ready to profit from your expertise and you want to know the first steps of how to do that.

Finally, this book is for you if you are like my dad was: you have skills and expertise but now need help positioning yourself as the expert that you know you are. You're smart, resourceful and good at what you do. You're perhaps both the most brilliant person anyone would hope to meet and the most talented person they've never heard of…yet.

INTRODUCTION

It's widely acknowledged that personal branding became a buzzphrase and actual career term after Tom Peters' 1997 Fast Company magazine article, *The Brand Called You*. In the decades since, dozens of marketing experts and public relations professionals alike have put more strategies around the scaffolding of Peters' concept.

With the internet making everyone with a Twitter account a global brand, the idea has taken on increased significance. Personal branding isn't an option - it's the default reality of today's global access to talent.

We are living in a digital age.

Our ability to access information and vet everyone from our accountant, to our kids' tutor is but a scroll and click away.

This means the world's ability to vet you is but a scroll and click away. When they search for you, what will they find? That's what this book sets out to answer and help you establish.

How the book is organized

Consider yourself a client, and me your public relations and personal branding coach. I've organized this book in a sequential format that mimics the ordered steps I'd take you through if you signed up to work with me one on one.

Step one is to get clear. We start with clarity of

your strengths, purpose and message. It's important to clarify your strengths because you need to understand the most compelling aspect of what you bring to the world. Not only that, you need to understand which of your gifts will be the cornerstone of your brand. I will guide you through the process of inquiry I personally use every year to determine my next direction and whether or not a service, product, relationship or other commitment is working. I advise others to reflect back on these questions annually at the very least. Once you are clear on your strengths and the value you bring to the world, we'll work to craft a clear message that communicates your passion and the value you present.

For step two, we'll work on creating the evidence and proof you need to back up your narrative and demonstrate that you're credible. The foundation of credibility must be established before we embark on promoting or monetizing your skills, talents, and ideas.

In step three, we'll define your big ideas. We'll work to uncover what you actually have to say through your thought leadership (yes, *you* have thought leadership). These ideas will guide how you show up on social media, in the media and on stages as a public speaker.

In step four, we'll help you get visible. Using the tools of online marketing and traditional marketing, we'll craft your plan to show up more visibly online, but also in person and through traditional channels like media and public speaking.

Last but certainly not least, we'll discuss how to sell yourself once you've done the work of figuring out who you are. And since this is a process you'll have to commit to for the long term, we'll outline how to make packaging your genius a realistic part of your daily life. I'll share productivity hacks that have worked for me and for clients as well as how to execute a plan to sell yourself year after year.

Ready?

Let's do this.

STEP 1
GET CLEAR ON YOUR BRAND

I can remember that morning so clearly. It was a few hours before my meeting with a new client, and I hadn't slept well.

I woke up only after hitting snooze on my 'wake up early', 'wake up on time', and 'wake up slightly late but still with enough time to hastily get dressed and out the door' alarms.

The rain didn't help any and I was feeling tired, groggy and decidedly un-ready for the world. I dropped my children off at their summer camp, then slowly drove to my office to get ready for the 10 a.m. session.

I couldn't shake the lethargy, and even coffee didn't help. As I watched the rain fall slowly and steadily, I considered rescheduling. But when I called into the conference line to do the session, something clicked.

This client was exciting to me and I had been looking forward to hearing the story of her 30+ year career in corporate fashion. She was ready to take the leap and go out on her own. She'd found me through a Google search and thought I could help her identify her target market and learn how to talk about herself and her skills.

I set out to do just that while remaining open to the unknown, and to possibilities of where our conversation could take us. You never know what will come up for people, what idea a question will spark, what train of thought they'll be inspired to follow. So from experience I've learned to release the expectations and just go where it goes.

Anyway, as we were wrapping up this nearly two hour session, the breakthroughs started coming rapid fire, one after another. She reflected that one particular idea explained an aspect of her personality that she hadn't been able to articulate her whole life. And to witness the clarity the realization fostered was exhilarating.

I hung up the phone *on fire*. I was amazed that just a few hours before I had been barely able to keep my eyes open.

But getting the chance to work for just a few hours in my purpose? That was like getting hit by a lightning bolt.

Pure energy.

Pay attention to what energizes you - it's the clearest indicator of your brand. If you're struggling to zero in on the work that makes you come alive, pay attention to moments like those. Pay attention to your lightning bolt moments. Pay attention to when you start your day on empty but somehow end it on full after getting filled up by your work.

That's your brand trying to communicate to you.

What excites you and gives you energy?

Whatever gets you physically and mentally energized is a huge clue to your brand and the starting point for working in your purpose.

You can have a resumé filled with important titles. You can have accolades for your achievements and testimonials referencing the amazing work you've done. You can have all these things and still not know who you are.

But your energy *can't* lie. It won't betray you. Your energy is a clue and a tool you can use to find the clarity that will focus your brand.

Remember your energy as you reflect on the first section of the book.

1

FACE YOUR GENIUS

RECONNECT WITH YOUR CHILDHOOD SELF

Growing up - when I was closest to myself - I was beyond confident in my writing abilities. Writing was the one thing I didn't hesitate about, because it wasn't really me - I was just a vessel.

Back then, if you put a pen in my hand, I went to another place. I couldn't tell you where the words came from, they just flowed - freely, generously, eloquently.

And it wasn't because I prepared to write. Sure, I got tons of "practice" by writing a lot, but it wasn't something that required preparation or work. It always felt as if the words were there waiting for me to summon them. That being the case, how could I take credit for simply being the channel through which they flowed?

Writing felt effortless and spiritual. I didn't have to think about it, I simply had to get out of the way so the words could find their way out. And for that reason, I always felt completely confident and assured. For the most part, I operated without hesitation whenever I had the opportunity to share my ideas or bare my soul through my writing.

I considered it my "gift" and felt grateful.

Over the years I have never felt like that about anything else professionally until I found this work. I realized that when I work with people one on one - call it coaching, call it mentoring, call it therapy - I can "prepare" all day and night but ultimately all I really need to do is show up and let the gift do the rest.

For a long time I struggled with that. Hearing people share their stories, listening for patterns, identifying false narratives, and holding a space for them to see themselves clearly just came so naturally to me. *'This can't be it,'* I thought. *'This is too easy. There must be more that I need to do to justify calling myself a coach or charging to do this thing that I do as easily as breathing...'*

After all, all I had to do was show up, get out of the way and allow myself to be a channel for the next person's breakthrough.

But that's the thing - when your gift is your gift, it is that easy.

Now, seeing what you bring to the table can be a difficult thing to do, especially since your true gift will typically feel so effortless. You can't dissect how you do it, because it comes so easily to you that you don't even realize that you are doing it half the time.

But I've learned it's not always about the doing so much as it is about the being: when are you being yourself and doing what you do best. As that happens, are you also being a vessel, a channel or a vehicle through which someone's change can travel?

That effortless state of being is purpose.

And you don't have to dress it up to sell it. You don't have to dilute the gift by overcomplicating it. You don't have to make yourself anxious perfecting and preparing yourself to justify it.

You just have to show up, get out of the way and allow yourself to be the channel that you are.

Questions to Consider

❖ What did you do for fun as a child?
❖ What were some of your childhood passions?
❖ What work feels easy to you, but difficult for others?
❖ What work do you feel guilty charging for?
❖ Where do you relax and lean into being so much that you don't realize what you're doing?
❖ What effortless work do others often compliment you on?

2
CLARIFY YOUR GENIUS
IDENTIFY YOUR STRENGTHS, SKILLS, AND THE VALUE YOU PROVIDE

After working for a decade in public relations, I began to incrementally pivot my skills and offer services as a "personal branding coach." I made this decision after noticing so many clients who had started coming to me for PR and marketing guidance. Eventually, I began to attract career changers and career climbers who needed my PR expertise. The influx of individual clientele encouraged me to open up my practice in order to be inclusive to both business owners and those figuring out their career paths.

As I continued to work with clients, a funny thing emerged. While many of the people came to me when they felt ready to package themselves and promote something in the world, I realized there were "prerequisites" to a successful personal branding process.

Before a client could authentically package and promote any aspect of who they were, they first needed to get clear on their values: why did they do what they did, what energized them? This pre-work would help ensure they were going down the right path.

During the course of my work, I realized that many people were packaging and promoting things that they weren't even really that passionate about. The high achievers who were most often drawn to me would typically excel in several different areas. Beyond lacking focus on which direction to go, they'd also find themselves getting pulled into different directions because smart outsiders saw their talents, and would intentionally steer the careers of these talented individuals.

I began speaking with clients who were blind to the magnitude of their talents and had no sense of direction for their gifts at all. It was all because they'd never had to strengthen their career compasses. They'd spent the majority of their careers on the receiving end of "favor" because someone or a series of someones had noticed them and said, "Oh, she's really good at math, so let me steer her in this direction..." or "Oh, she's an incredible analytical thinker. Let me see if I can move her into consulting, or maybe she can work under me and help me build my empire..."

If this sounds like you, this is your chance to finally take the time to do a serious process of self-discovery. This book will help you think through the purpose of your gifts, the direction you want to take your talents, and how you want to use your unique skills in this lifetime.

I'm a big believer in looking at the clues of what's already working in your life or your business and building from there. What are your common themes? Who do you always gravitate to? Who always gravitates to you? Can you duplicate a past success? Can you create success around an area of promise?

One of my goals for this book is to help you understand what makes you tick as well as what some of your roadblocks are. I also want you to understand what is working in your career or your business, as well as some of the clues you may be overlooking.

In my experience, the answers are already there, this process is simply here to help you uncover them. While I plan to lay out a process for you to follow, it will only work if you are open to it.

Strengthening your internal compass

I'm a champion of getting back in touch with yourself, your passions, and rediscovering your strengths.

When we were children, we didn't need help determining our personal brands - we knew *instinctively* what we were all about. We *lived* our personal brands just by being ourselves. But somewhere along the way, many of us forgot how to do that. We lost sight of our magic. We fell into the routines of life, were programmed by well-meaning parents and teachers to follow rules, wait for instruction and ignore what was happening internally.

Sound familiar?

If you're like most people I work with, you're either a business owner longing for more purpose in your work, or an employee looking to leave your current role because you realize you can't go on like this forever. And by 'go on like this' I mean continue down a path that isn't going anywhere. This could look like a job that fell into your lap, a client you took on only because you needed the money, or a leadership position you took out of obligation after being recommended by a smart mentor who recognized your talents.

Many of the people I work with have multiple talents and skills. The problem arises when we mistake our talents and skills with our purpose. Just because you're good at something doesn't mean that's what you're supposed to be doing with your time.

We've all experienced jobs, clients, etc. that were not the right fit. But if we look back and are honest with ourselves, we knew all along they weren't. We just didn't listen to ourselves and trust our own judgment.

Your life's assignment

The Package Your Genius process offers you a way to get back in tune with your own judgement just as you did as a child.

What does this have to do with your personal brand? Well, if you are in touch with yourself and who you really are, you'll be able to get that much closer to the real purpose and assignment for your life. You'll then be able to clearly communicate that to the people it can serve. Instead of trying to fit yourself into a box, when you package your genius, you unleash your magic. And I assure you, nothing feels better than that.

Set an intention to reconnect with your intuition as it will guide you not only back to what you want, but also toward what you're meant to be doing with your gifts. Here's an overview of the questions you want to ask:

❖ Who are you?
❖ What are your strengths?
❖ What is your solution?
❖ Who is your audience?
❖ What is your mode of working?

Let's dive into the questions.

The BIG Question

Who are you?

How do you know who you are? One proven way to answer the question is to first identify your strengths. Now, I won't turn this into a book on strengths because there are dozens of wonderful books on that topic, but I will share an overview of how to figure it out, as well as a few tools that will help you.

Why strengths? I firmly believe that your strengths are your **truth mirrors**; they're the windows into your authenticity. Strengths are like the cardinal directions of your internal compass. If it's grown too quiet and you can't quite hear your internal voice anymore, your strengths are fantastic guideposts.

So how do we find our strengths? There are internal and external clues.

Internal clues to your strengths

First, let's talk about the internal clues. What brings you alive? What *energizes* you? What do you look forward to doing? When do you feel a sense of flow?

Practically speaking, you can look at what Michael Bungay Stanier described in his book *Do More Great Work* as "peak moments." Essentially, you want to look back over your working life and begin cataloging those moments when you felt physically energized by your work.

Marcus Buckingham talks about a similar sensation in his book *Go Put Your Strengths to Work*. Buckingham asks readers to make a list of things they loved and things they loathed. Not surprisingly, when it comes to your working life, those 'loved it' moments are a clue to your most natural strengths.

Take a minute to jot down a few of the peak moments that you've experienced in your career. If you're hard pressed to think of any career peak moments, think back to a time when you were doing purposeful work either in the community, your church, with your family, or even in school. You'll be referencing those later.

Another way to get closer to your strengths is to zero in on the parts of your work that drain you. The problem with focusing solely on your strengths is you can make the mistake of solving the *right* problem for the *wrong* audience, approaching the *right* audience with the *wrong* solution, or delivering the *right* solution in the *wrong* format.

Basically, if you only focus on your strengths you may end up with work that takes you almost to the fulfillment line, but stops short and feels incomplete. For example, you may see that something is working well for another person in your industry. Even if they seem to be having a great time with it, in time you may come to realize that what works for them may not work for you because what energizes them may drain you and vice versa.

Take a second to think about what **drains** you. Think about your current tasks, colleagues, or clients. There may be aspects of the work you enjoy even though other parts drain you. These are things you'll want to automate, delegate or avoid altogether.

What drains you about your work?

Finding your strengths externally

After you spend some time doing the self reflection that only you can do to identify your internal clues of your strengths, then it's time to look at your external clues. The external clues can be found by asking yourself another series of questions.

First, what do people thank you for? This is one of my very favorite questions to ask because most people don't think about it at all. Far too many of us are oblivious to the gratitude we receive from others, yet gratitude is a tremendous indicator of where others are receiving value from us. I'm of the opinion that you cannot plan to grow your audience or expect people to promote you or pay for your services if you don't first add value to their lives.

Next question: what do people always ask for your help with? This is the opposite side of the gratitude question. If you have a hard time remembering the last time you received gratitude (or maybe the people in your life are largely ungrateful, which is another problem altogether) think instead about what people *ask for your help* with. For many people, that's a much easier question to tackle.

The great thing about this question is that it typically shows up in every area of your life, if you think broadly enough.

For example, as a coach I am typically responsible for helping people activate something new in their lives. That could mean launching a new brand podcast, igniting a business or getting started with a new book project. Not so ironically, I'm also tasked with 'getting the ball rolling' at home. Whenever it's time to move a big project forward, I'm typically the person those in my family or circle of friends turn to. In that way, I'm asked to help activate new ideas and am thanked for being the catalyst for major changes.

Where do you receive consistent gratitude across all areas of your life? What contribution do people consistently thank you for?

Look at what's working

You now know how to go about examining the internal and external clues to your strengths. But there are more ways to examine the direction your personal brand should take.

Look at your life - what's working? What is really working well? Reflect back on the past year, or for those of you who have been in your field for a while, the total length of your career. Reflect on your professional roles and community involvement. What's working well for you at work?

When you can identify your strengths, what energizes you and what the world is already mirroring back to you in the form of gratitude, clarity is inevitable for both you and the audience with whom you plan to connect.

Your purpose? Or someone else's?

Strong personal brands are rooted in a keen sense of self-awareness. Memorable people exude a sense of knowing who they are, what they want and exactly where they are going.

Yet so many people don't know where they're going because they've delegated the leadership in their lives - someone else is steering their ship.

So many of us spend years denying our true interests and strengths in favor of following a path directed by people whose approval we crave. It's the choice to go to law school over becoming a writer. Or to study medicine instead of becoming a business owner or artist because that was the prestigious path a parent wanted. It could even be staying in a current position because it's secure and other people say you're lucky to have your job and you're crazy to want to do something different.

Maybe you've made great grades, earned multiple degrees, landed coveted positions, and become indispensable to your employer. And yet, fulfillment is nowhere to be found because the path chosen doesn't align with your internal motivators.

To start steering your ship again, first take a look back to the clues left by a school-aged you. What intrigued you? What lit you on fire? Who and what inspired you? Then reflect back on the last time you felt like you were operating 100% in your zone. What were you doing?

The same way it's easy to allow a parent or spouse to steer your ship, it's also easy to fall trap to well-meaning mentors and others. At some point in your journey, you may need to ask yourself if your talents are serving your purpose or someone else's?

As a high achiever, you know you're talented. But when you're talented, it's even more important to understand what YOU want to do. Smart people, observing your gifts, will always find a way to utilize you. So if you're not clear on the direction you want your career and work to take, others will steer your talents towards their own benefit. And if you're not careful, you will wake up one day having done many meaningful things that meant nothing to you.

Congratulations!

You've just survived the first phase of the process - which is a pretty substantial lesson. Don't make the mistake of rushing through this very important work!

Questions to Consider

- ❖ When do you feel energized?
- ❖ What do people thank you for?
- ❖ What do people ask for your help with? What problem do you solve for your audience?
- ❖ Are you steering your own ship?
- ❖ Are you working towards your purpose or someone's else's vision for your gifts and talents?

3

COMMUNICATE YOUR GENIUS

PACKAGE A BRAND MESSAGE THAT CONNECTS

During chapter two, you focused on getting clarity on what energizes you and what value you currently bring to the world. In this chapter, we'll tease out the components of a brand message that outlines the problem you solve and the audience you solve that problem for.

The purpose of framing your message this way is simple: the more people can understand the problem you solve, the more opportunities you'll attract to engage with the people you were designed to help.

Problems you solve

Most people wouldn't think to frame an elevator pitch in terms of the problems they solve. Yet problem solving is critical because whatever you have to offer is a solution to someone's problem.

Whether you own your own business, run your own department or aspire to run for office, *you are a solution*. Your potential customers, audience members, or employers are looking for solutions, and your message should explain how you are that missing piece.

For example, one of my clients is a productivity expert and executive coach. She helps busy working mothers make the big decisions that impact the family for months and years to come. She helps high performing, high achieving women move beyond the paralysis of indecision, identify the next best step to take and finally get into action. Her coaching helps women unlock progress and typically sets off a chain reaction of events that generates momentum in the home.

As a problem solver, she helps women who struggle to narrow down their choices and make firm decisions. She helps procrastinators choose a course of action and set big projects in motion.

What about you? What problems do you currently solve? What problems do people always ask you to solve but you aren't solving? What problems would you like to solve?

When you can tie your narrative to the problems you solve for an audience, the easier it will be to sell yourself and make your brand memorable to them.

What audience has the problem you solve?

The word 'tribe' is one that is thrown around a lot, especially in the online space. The word evokes the idea of followers, believers, and true fans. You may not feel that you have a tribe, but trust me, you do. It just may not look like the tribe of a well-known influencer or celebrity…yet.

When I think about a tribe, I want to know where are you *already* influential? Where do you already know lots of people? Where do people know you? Where do you have traction? Where are you trusted? This is important to note because this is where you should expend most of your energy in the beginning of your brand building efforts. If you know what works, you can build on what's working until you feel the need to pivot.

For example, when I first opened my services up and began to offer coaching and strategy sessions, I realized how many people I knew working in the communications and media industry. At first, this seemed problematic; I essentially wanted to offer public relations services and my network was comprised mainly of other public relations people! *Yikes!* But it worked out that many of my first coaching clients were independent public relations professionals who needed help marketing themselves in order to get clients.

Even if it seems counterintuitive, who is attracted to you? It may be a new audience, or an audience you've yet to address. Is there someone whom you haven't given yourself permission to work with, but they keep coming around to work with you?

Demographic niches

When you examine the type of clients you attract, what do they have in common? Do they all fit into a racial or age-based demographic, for example black millennial women? Do they fit into a career or professional demographic, i.e. female attorneys at top-tier law firms, or my earlier example of mid-level communications and media professionals? Do they fit into a lifestyle demographic group like suburban gymnastics parents or divorced golfers?

You can get as specific as you like. If I were to narrow my early career niche, I might identify sub-niches like independent public relations practitioners, non-profit communications professionals, corporate communications professionals, or entry-level communications professionals as each group has different concerns.

If you take "suburban moms" as a niche, you can break that down further into suburban soccer moms vs. suburban lacrosse moms, or suburban stay-at-home moms vs. suburban working moms. You could even specify different aspects of the niche depending on your goals by focusing on a location. Consider the following examples:

Suburban Lacrosse Moms of McLean, Virginia
Suburban Mompreneurs of America
Suburban Toddler Moms and Tea Aficionados

Situational niches

Another way to look at who you attract is to profile the people who most often ask you for help. Don't make the mistake of ignoring who usually raises their hand to work with you.

Note: *this will likely evolve over time.* This may have already changed since the first time you worked on building your brand. You are ever evolving, which is why what used to energize you may not energize you as much anymore, and that's okay.

When you find that what energized you then doesn't anymore, it's simply a sign that you need to go through the inventory of questions in the first part of the chapter again and begin to plot your pivot.

Your mode of working

When you feel you're at your most effective and most fulfilled, how are you working?

This is important. Nobody can beat you when you're doing what you do best in the mode you were born to do it! Pay attention to those peak moments when you light up – how are you working?

For example: My natural mode is writing alone, and sharing to the masses – I've always had strong writing skills since I was a child. It brings me great joy and is extremely energizing when I can connect with someone who's read my words and experienced a personal breakthrough.

As you explore your natural mode, ask yourself whether you are naturally extroverted and a strong speaker, or do you get your point across better in writing?

Do you get energy from large groups of people, or do you prefer to work one on one? Everyone's mode is different. But that's the beauty of this process – when you package your genius, you'll find what you come up with is tailored specifically to you.

Mode of genius - more examples:

- leading
- managing
- inspiring
- writing
- connecting people
- speaking
- explaining
- teaching
- training
- consulting
- performing
- demonstrating
- networking
- socializing

The previous list covers what you're doing when you're at your best. But don't forget to think about how you are working when you're at your best. For example, are you working one on one, in a small group, with a large group, behind the scenes, in solitude, from the stage. This is where your personal style and take comes into play. I have always enjoyed uncovering my insights in solitude before explaining and encouraging people with those insights in small groups or one on one.

Crafting the narrative

Once you understand your audience, mode of working and solution, it's your job to make sure that your audience knows exactly what you do - exactly the problem that you solve. Your brand message isn't simply a job title. On the contrary, it is a clear and concise narrative that explicitly says who and how you help.

For example - *I'm a health and wellness professional with a certification in integrative nutrition* becomes, *I'm a health and wellness advisor for the modern woman. I help physically inactive women who hate to exercise find the physical activity they can joyfully integrate to their busy lifestyle so they can reach optimal health while having fun.*

You get the idea. Ultimately, you need to make your 'about me' narrative less about you and more about your *audience*. You want your audience to see themselves and their problem in your narrative. It's all fine and good to impress others with your degrees and awards, but ultimately your audience wants to know if you can help them.

Questions to Consider

- ❖ What problem do you solve?
- ❖ What is your narrative?
- ❖ Who naturally gravitates to you or requests your help?
- ❖ When you feel energized by your work, what are you doing?
- ❖ What work format usually brings out your best?
- ❖ What people are easy and effortless to help?

STEP 2
MAKE THE CASE

Early in my public relations career, I knew I needed to reach a broader audience if I wanted my business to grow. I decided that a good step for me to take would be to write for a national business publication to expand my exposure. I was steadily building my list of media contacts, and I had been writing consistently 2-3 times per week on my own blog.

I reached out to an editor friend and requested the opportunity to write for his magazine. In my pitch, I included links to the types of stories I could produce - these were pieces I'd already published on my own blog so the editor just had to click through to see my writing style and determine whether or not I was a good fit.

Within a few weeks, I was offered a regular writing position for the magazine - a widely circulated, national business publication - I was thrilled!

Since then, I've counseled many clients on how to land guest writing opportunities as well as media commentary of course. I often reflect back on the experience of pitching myself to get that first business column. The process is really the same for making any good pitch - whether you're trying to secure a media segment or a promotion.

Before you pitch yourself for a next level opportunity, the first thing you'll need is a portfolio: **evidence** of past work that show what you've done. You'll need to demonstrate your past capabilities if you want the person you're pitching to take you seriously.

How can you make the case for your brand? How can you illustrate what you've already done? What evidence do you have to support a new opportunity? Ponder these questions as you learn to make the case for your gifts in the next two chapters.

Before you ask someone to give you an opportunity, come armed with evidence to support your request.

Then go ahead and shoot your shot!

4
RECEIPTS

SHOWCASE EVIDENCE OF YOUR WORK AND VALUE

It's time to take your narrative to the next level and tie it to what we've done. You've examined how you help and who you help; now it's time to deepen that message with some specific examples of your past work and the value you add.

Now's the time to establish your credibility.

Why is evidence important?

Evidence is important because people need to know what you've done in order to have confidence in what you can do. Think about it: it's not enough to say who you are, or what you do. You also need to give others an idea of what you can do by illustrating what you have done in the past.

And unlike most personal branding philosophies in the marketplace, packaging your genius is about more than just *saying* what you can do. It's about communicating where you're already credible and why you deserve new opportunities. Evidence helps you to engage an audience and get new people to buy in to your pitch. You may have your expertise nailed down, but until you can demonstrate some sort of track record, you're going to have a difficult time selling that genius to an audience who is not yet familiar with you.

But evidence is also critical for *you.* As a high achiever, you may have fallen into the trap of immersing yourself completely in doing great work. You've likely made it your priority to do a good job, to produce great results and keep your head down. And in the doing, it becomes easy to forget what it's all adding up to; it becomes easy to forget what you've done and who you've become in the process of all that doing.

You know the drill: you have a a big team win, or you take a client to new heights and you immediately move on to the next thing. A year or more can pass and those big accomplishments quickly fade to memories.

If you don't intentionally take time to assess yourself and your wins regularly, you can't know how valuable you are in the marketplace. And if you don't know how valuable you are, it's harder to make the case for new opportunities. And if you do get the chance to pitch yourself, you likely won't demand what you're worth.

If you are looking to attract more opportunities in the next five years (who isn't?!) do yourself a favor and set a personal calendar reminder to assess yourself and any new contributions to add to your narrative at least twice each year. Take some time now to asses what you've done and what you uniquely bring to the table so you can negotiate from a position of power when the time comes.

Communicating evidence of your work

Before we talk about how to go about finding the evidence you need, let me share a few ways that you can communicate evidence to your audiences:

- narrative case studies about your professional experience, client milestones, board work, client work or volunteer work
- speaking clips
- writing samples
- photos and videos
- creative portfolio

Whatever you want more of will determine the type of evidence you need. In terms of building your personal brand, you may want more speaking engagements, media attention or what most of us want - more clients! But depending on what you want, that will determine the type of evidence that you need.

For example, a university professor looking to build her brand as a national media commentator and thought leader on her topic may want more national television opportunities. In order to land those more coveted media appearances, evidence for her may take the form of local television or national online media clips that show where she's already solidified herself as an expert on her broader topic.

Or, a coach for women entrepreneurs may want

to speak at a popular, and highly selective international entrepreneurs summit. When applying to speak for this national event, she may be asked to list past speaking opportunities where she's successfully spoken to an audience of business women. In this case, she'd have to provide a list of those past engagements, and she may also need to provide speaking references as well.

Another example - when an executive coaching client of mine was ready to pivot his experience from nonprofit to government to corporate, we noticed that a common thread from all of his work was his ability to engage stakeholders and facilitate partnerships. So we developed case studies that illustrated how he'd done that in the nonprofit and government spaces with partners that corporations were looking to work with as well. He packaged a clear narrative about his nonprofit experience and successfully pitched himself to a corporate environment.

While this specific transition from nonprofit to corporate can prove to be a challenge for many, it was straightforward for him because he could clearly articulate what he'd done in a way that made the case for his value to a corporation.

Think about **your** experience. How can you communicate what you've done in the past so that others will know what you can do for them? What type of evidence do you need to illustrate that you are qualified and positioned to add value? Where can you communicate this evidence?

Transitioning

You may be transitioning or building your brand on a new foundation where you don't have a ton of specific expertise yet. That's okay. Relax. We are going to pinpoint exactly the *type* of evidence you'll need to get in order to make this part of your personal brand come to life.

I've been doing this work long enough to know that some of you are reading this and thinking to yourself: *What if I don't have evidence?* Ah…but I will argue that you do. You have *something* that translates into your personal brand or else you wouldn't be building a brand around it.

Take the example of a personal trainer who may want to start offering meal-planning services. She may not have a ton of direct meal-planning clients yet, but if she has suggested healthy meal ideas for clients and family members and they have seen success, evidence can be developed from that.

If the topic you're building your personal brand upon is totally new territory, it may be time for you to volunteer to get the evidence you need. That may mean identifying people who fit the profile of your target audience and offering them complimentary services for the sole purpose of creating a narrative around how you helped them. It may look like serving on a committee in another department at work or volunteering to help out on a project outside of your current scope to get the experience you need.

Where to find evidence

Think back to the previous chapter when you identified peak moments, or those moments when you were doing work that made you feel alive. What did you identify as a peak moment? Can that be developed into a case study or piece of evidence?

Another place to look would be your extraordinary outputs. So if assigning "peak moment" to an experience seem like high praise, think about the times you definitely got some good results.

For example, early in my public relations days, I often shopped around a case study that showcased my integrated marketing and communications results for a nonprofit client. While I did enjoy the project, I didn't consider it a peak moment. However, it was a clear example of my digital media skills and ability to make things happen for clients. I successfully used that one case study to secure a ton of other nonprofit client work.

Another place to look for evidence is in those 'thank you' moments. What have been some of the big projects your clients, friends, colleagues or even mentees have thanked you for? Even if you don't see the results you provided as a 'big deal', remember: if you received gratitude you likely added value.

Make a list of 3-5 examples that you can use to build case studies that demonstrate your expertise.

Case studies are a great way to show what you've done. But before you set out to capture your evidence, it's important that you strive to create a narrative format because as any good marketer will tell you, stories sell.

I'm going to break down the simple four paragraph formula format to get a killer case study that sells whatever you're trying to sell.

Crafting the case study

In paragraph one, you want to establish the situation. Start with the company, customer, client, or object of the case study. What was the situation? Where were they before you began your work with them? What problem were they experiencing? How dire were the straits? Paint a picture of what this problem looked like and its implications. What was at stake? What was it costing the organization?

In paragraph two, you'll share your observations upon starting the work. Remember, this is a narrative, so you need to tell a story. After you've painted the picture of the situation, you'll want to share a part of your thought process and strategic thinking. What did you observe about the situation? Did you agree with the company or client about the real cause of their problem? Did you have ideas about a new approach? Once you've established the situation your subject was in, describe your starting point for working with them, and how you determined your approach.

In paragraph three you will detail your approach, what you did. How did you tackle the problem? In this paragraph, share your methodology, or your step-by-step approach to solving the problem. What did you do first, second, and third? How did you start?

Eventually, how did you wrap up the work?

Finally, in paragraph four you'll reveal the outcomes of your work. What were the results? What happened? What changes did the client see? Think about the numbers you can use to quantify those results. Can you share information about the number of pounds lost, or the percentage increase in web traffic? Can you point to a specific number of new opportunities? Be sure to communicate in terms of specific tangible outcomes.

Showcasing your evidence

After you've taken the time to thoughtfully examine your past results and craft narratives around them, you're probably wondering exactly where do you put this evidence? Depending on your personal brand and your specific objectives, there are a few places you can showcase them.

Linkedin

If you've fully developed your Linkedin profile, you'll notice the room after you list each career role. I call these "Linkedin position descriptions" and you can add details of your narrative case studies there. You want to use case studies in your position descriptions instead of your summary because you need room to specify evidence for each role.

Your web site

If you use a web site to market yourself or your services, you can create a page on your web site called 'portfolio,' 'client results,' 'work samples,' or even 'case studies' depending on the nature of your work to showcase your evidence. Believe me, these case studies really do help to sell your work especially if you're doing transformative work like coaching or consulting that aims to help a client move the needle on one particular aspect of their lives or business.

Sales pages

If you sell products or programs, at some point you may need to set up a sales page that sells your latest offering. In addition to testimonials from clients (which we'll cover in the next chapter) case studies can be a great way for your to market the effectiveness of your work.

Marketing documents and proposals

Depending on the type of work you do and the type of work you want, in-depth case studies may be a great way to wow potential clients.

As I mentioned before, when I did longterm digital media engagements for organizations, I routinely sent out case studies to give potential clients a taste for the type of results I could get for them. I would attach the case studies as pdf files and send them shortly after meeting a new business contact. I now add a case studies section to corporate proposals.

Interviews and performance reviews

The true purpose of a case study is to capture evidence of your work in a way that is easy to remember and share.

If you're job hunting, having a few case studies top of mind will go a long way when it's time to sit down and sell yourself during an interview.

Even if you don't feel the need to write out four paragraphs and post them anywhere, by jotting down your own notes on the four phases of an effective case study - the situation, your observations, your methodology, your results - you will be able to master any conversation where you and your skills are being evaluated for a new opportunity.

Using evidence to pivot

Now it should be noted, your work is about solving a problem in some way. Your evidence points to your credibility to create change. But understand that you can pivot your personal brand and position yourself to do something new based on new evidence.

If you are struggling with how your past informs your present, think about the linkages or parallels that exist between what you've done and what you want to do.

Future-focused evidence: be intentional

Once I met with a mentee to discuss her plans for a newly procured summer internship. While she reported feeling excited about the opportunity to learn and improve her skills, she was feeling unsupported by her internship advisor, as there wasn't much guidance there. She wasn't sure what she was supposed to be doing, or what she was supposed to be learning during her summer experience.

But she was excited because even though her advisors weren't clear (they were busy managing the day to day of their business) she was inadvertently put in a position to interface with insiders in an industry she desperately wanted to break into.

I asked her about her goals for her summer experience. She said she didn't know. "Well," I mused, "since your advisors clearly aren't in a position to spoon feed you, why not set your own goals for the summer? Why not *decide* that this opportunity won't be worth your time unless you walk away with a.) five new industry connections that you can potentially cultivate longterm as mentors and future employers, b.) one new process that you can say you can do from start to finish (i.e. conceptualize, launch and measure a 30 day social media campaign,) and c.) a glowing recommendation from your internship advisor?"

In other words - get some goals, and get them quickly!

Suddenly, she got excited. She hadn't thought that she could be so strategic. After all, she was just a 20 year old college student who was lucky to land an internship.

Not so.

I told her that her time is the one asset that she can't get back. So she should choose how she spends it wisely.

But as I thought about it, I began to give her more examples of how a clear cut goal can improve the prospects of getting good evidence from a myriad of situations. Before networking events, conferences and coffee dates, I always try to identify my takeaways - what do I want to walk away from this experience with? Sometimes it is as specific as a new client or a scheduled meeting. Other times, it's the desire to deepen a relationship with someone I may not often see but want to get to know better. But I always have a goal or two in mind. And even when I don't meet my goals, I always feel quite satisfied knowing that I'm closer than I would have been had I not set any.

What about you? Are you setting goals for how you spend your time? Before you hit that conference or networking reception, have you decided who you want to meet or have a conversation with?

Maybe the job you're currently in isn't a perfect fit, but could it somehow put you in proximity to something better? Even if your current situation isn't ideal, what goals can you set for your time so that you walk away smarter, richer, better connected or more marketable for the next opportunity with evidence that supports your goals?

I'm a big believer in creative visualization - the idea that what you focus on will grow because it's real. When you get intentional about the outcomes you want to see, the opportunities to achieve those outcomes become crystal clear.

So don't just accept what comes your way. Be intentional and strategic. How can you turn a less than perfect situation into an opportunity to create evidence?

Upgrade your self-image

After mining your past for stories, and with the full landscape of your career set out before you, it may become clear where you've been underselling yourself. Seeing the clear impact of your work and the value your gifts and talents have created for others, you may be kicking yourself for not asking for more all along!

If you find yourself in this situation, ask yourself does your self-image need an upgrade? If you have been on a particular career path for some time, it's easy and perhaps normal to fall into the trap of thinking that you are who you used to be, and can only get what you used to get.

But what has happened to you over the last year, five years, or even in the last decade? What new accomplishments have you not yet included in your personal brand story that could help you make the case for more?

You are not who you were when you first started out. You're not the same person you where when you evaluated yourself or pitched yourself five years ago.

Your pricing, salary, positioning and confidence in your professional experience should reflect who you are, not who you used to be.

Questions to Consider

- ❖ What are 3-5 specific experiences you can develop case studies around?
- ❖ Who have you worked with and who you want to work with?
- ❖ What evidence can you extract from those you've worked with?
- ❖ How can you use your evidence to translate your experience into something new?
- ❖ If there is no link, how will you go about getting the evidence you need to make your case?
- ❖ What does your current evidence say about you? What story does it tell?
- ❖ Is the story you're telling through your current evidence in alignment with your ultimate goals?

5
LET OTHERS TALK
SECURE INVALUABLE SOCIAL PROOF

If evidence consists of you sharing your own account of how you got results, social proof then is hearing what happened from the other side.

There are a few types of social proof, among them recommendations, testimonials, endorsements, ratings and reviews.

For physicians and doctors in private practice, there are a number of sites that you can encourage clients to post to after they have a session with you. If there is a niche site that resonates with your clients or your industry, by all means send people there to rate you.

But we're going to focus on LinkedIn recommendations because they're ubiquitous, and most everyone can use them to build social proof for your personal brand. If you have a web site, you can also use those recommendations as testimonials for your site, provided that you ask for that permission up front.

Who can recommend you?

If you're thinking that no one would recommend you, you couldn't be more wrong! Regardless of where you are in your career or business journey, you likely have several people who can vouch for your value.

What colleagues, supervisors or directors are most familiar with your work? If you sit on a nonprofit board, the executive director of the nonprofit would be a great person to ask. If you work with clients in a coaching or consultative capacity, your past and current clients may be great sources for recommendations. If you create content - say you run a blog, podcast or write books - your audience members are great sources to tap.

Think back to our discussion of what you want more of. If you want more speaking engagements, you would do well to highlight your past speaking clients, and solicit recommendations from people who have hired you to speak in the past.

Other examples:
- Mentors and mentees
- College professors and department heads
- Editors who publish your writing online
- Champions from your past - we all have them

Don't be afraid to reach out!

How to request LinkedIn recommendations

First, make sure you customize your recommendation request in LinkedIn. Don't use the default template.

Second, when you make your ask, be sure to mention the specific aspect of your work that you want your colleague to reference.

For example, after one speaking engagement, an executive at the company mentioned that I was one of the most engaging speakers they'd had in some time. Their audience was excited to hear from me, as my message helped create a big shift for many of the people in the room. When I reached out for a recommendation, I used that exact language in my request.

Basically, you want to make it easy on the person recommending you because they may not remember exactly what they said or what aspect of your work to talk about. They may, but then again they may not. Your job is to make it as easy for them as possible.

A great time to request recommendations is when you're talking to a client or reader in person. Most people are more effusive when speaking than when they're writing, so get them talking if you can. If you don't have a voice recorder or it would be inappropriate to request to record the conversation (use your best judgement) try to jot down the gist of their sentiments so you can type it up later. Then shortly after seeing them in person, send your request and mention that you took the liberty of typing up some of their recent remarks as an option.

I have done this for several clients who I know are extremely busy, or are not strong writers. I have also done it for well known influencers who likely get many of these requests. For one such influencer, I took the initiative to write up a recommendation myself because I knew she wouldn't take the time to do it, even though she was telling me how much that I have helped her. When I heard her glowing praise, I took notes, paraphrased what she said, and typed it up.

Voilà.

When to request recommendations

If possible, you want to request recommendations when you're reaching a milestone or wrapping up a significant project or on a high note. It's much easier to request these recommendations when the energy is high, not when things are stale, too much time has passed, or the person recommending you doesn't remember the details of your work together.

However, if it's been years since you were in touch with someone, still reach out. It's still worth it to try. In the best case scenario, you'll want to be proactive.

Other great times to reach out to people for recommendations:
- after you represent your company well publicly - on a panel, or after a series of company-wide events
- after you speak at a conference, and you got rave reviews
- after you launch a book and someone says they read it and loved it
- after you host a successful workshop and your

participants are full of breakthroughs
- after you complete a stellar client engagement

Don't wait until you are leaving your job or are down to your last client to start reaching out to people from your past. Make it a practice to do it regularly. I like to schedule time in my calendar to think about who I can reach out to quarterly, or twice per year at the very least.

Questions to Consider

❖ Who are your brand or career champions?
❖ Who holds you in high regard and regularly speaks in glowing terms about you?
❖ Who can enthusiastically recommend your work?
❖ Who can speak to the contribution you are capable of making to another organization?
❖ What work and projects do you need to secure recommendations for?

STEP 3
DEFINE YOUR BIG IDEAS

Shortly after I graduated from college, I wrote an article that changed my life.

I remember taking my first Apple laptop with me to the newly opened Starbucks on U Street in Washington, and sitting down to write.

At the time, U Street (and the whole District of Columbia) was transforming. The thoroughfare which had once been affectionately referred to as "Black Broadway" was changing before my eyes. I noticed that in the midst of constructing new condominiums, a beautiful mural of Duke Ellington had been taken down. The fact that the new condo building was going to be named "The Ellington" was more than I could take.

Fueled by Starbucks lattes and my youthful exuberance, I hammered out an essay on U Street, Duke Ellington, and my complicated feelings about gentrification. It was not lost on me that I was enjoying the first harbinger of gentrification on the block - a brand new Starbucks store - while simultaneously missing a relic of the neighborhood's past.

I wrote the essay and emailed the book editor at the Washington Post. I only had her information because she was my former English Professor's sister and some months before had agreed to meet me for an informational interview. She sent my essay to the editor of the Outlook section who agreed to take a look.

Fast forward about a month later, that essay was published in the Sunday issue of the Washington Post, setting off a series of very fortunate events for me. I had never published anything before, so to have my first piece published in the Post was huge. I didn't have a website and there was no Twitter at the time. I only had an email address which was included with my byline. I had never received so many emails prior to that article's publication.

Seeing the response to my writing was exhilarating, and it pushed me to seek out other opportunities to feel that same euphoria. I got serious about freelancing, and with my one precious clip in hand, I pounded the pavement to find other opportunities to write and publish.

I scored two freelance reporting gigs at small local newspapers, and proceeded to build up my writing clips. Once I had enough good stories, I submitted them for a journalism fellowship at Northwestern University's Medill School - a fellowship I'd previously been rejected for.

But this time I was accepted. I got the fellowship, spent a glorious summer writing in Chicago, then came back to DC and began writing for the Washington City Paper. I saw myself following in the footsteps of my two writing idols at the time - Kate Boo and Ta-Nehisi Coates - who had also once been staff writers there.

Things were going well until I lost my newspaper job at the beginning of the Great Recession. Luckily for me, I never lost my desire to write. I flipped journalism into communications and used my writing skills to help tell nonprofit and small business stories.

I craved my own creative outlet, so I started a blog. The internet was heating up and big publications like the Washington Post were no longer the only way to publish one's ideas. So I blogged about working in communications after journalism, how social media seemed like it was going to be a big thing, and what I was learning about online tools.

As a new mom who didn't get out much, I made friends online and connected with other communications colleagues. I shared my journey and shared what I was learning through my blog. Just by sharing, I inadvertently became a teacher and built a personal brand in the process.

Looking back, I owe my business and brand to writing. What started as a fortuitous post in a national publication fueled an entire business...

I wouldn't be where I am today without the ability to publish my ideas whenever I choose. And it wouldn't be nearly as easy for my clients to find me online. I am so grateful.

The same can be true for you. Whether you just write the first 5 posts for your company blog or start sharing your ideas more regularly on LinkedIn, the resulting body of work can establish your brand securely within your topic of expertise.

When people research you and find your ideas, they'll know you're the real deal. Keep this in mind as you absorb the following chapters.

6

WHAT TO SHARE

UNCOVER YOUR THOUGHT LEADERSHIP

Thought leadership is a term that gets thrown a lot, but for our purposes, I'm defining it as the set of ideas you will share when you embrace the mantle of expert, in the area of your choosing.

Now let me be clear: by deciding to out yourself as an expert, you're not proclaiming to know everything on your topic. You are however, an expert on your unique personal experience as it relates to that topic, and that is something no one can dispute.

No one else is an expert on your experience.

A common stumbling block for those on the personal brand building continuum is the reluctance to break from the ranks of the crowd and assume their rightful position as leader.

Stuck in student mode

I come across many intelligent, talented, capable people who are sitting in the classroom long past the point when they should have been leading the class.

They're stuck in "student mode" and refuse to own their expertise. They can't seem to step up and graduate into their earned identity as leader, despite having so much to share.

On the other hand, I also come across those who have been long elevated as leaders and teachers, so they're comfortable with the "expert" identity. And unfortunately, that comfort keeps them standing in front of the class when they should be taking a seat to learn!

It's a cyclical phenomenon. As you learn and grow, your identity will evolve over and over again. One day, you're the clueless student eager to soak up knowledge like a sponge. But if you stay in that space long enough, just like a sponge, your understanding will become saturated and you won't be able to effectively hold any excess. At that point it's time to move to the front of the class and teach, or move on.

Self promotion behind the scenes

One of the most frustrating things about being a "behind the scenes" person is being able to effectively market the ideas of others, while not being able to harness your marketing powers for yourself.

You are likely accustomed to communicating ideas on behalf of others. You know how to craft an idea. You may even be persuasive, or know how to write well.

The challenge emerges when it's time to turn the marketing mirror on yourself. How do you talk about what you do in a way that helps you reach your goals? How do you put on the "expert" hat and begin communicating from that perspective? How do you come out from behind the scenes and start jumping into industry conversations - not on behalf of a boss or client, but on behalf of yourself? How do you conquer your fear of self promotion, and come across in a way that is true to yourself?

Even if you're not in the marketing or communications field, the idea of having no problem playing a "behind the scenes" role likely resonates. If you have no problem sharing information about friends and family, promoting the expertise of your clients, your boss, your team, your CEO or Executive Director but struggle to share your ideas from the perspective of expert, here are three starting points to help you take the first step.

Where do you have more to add?

Begin to notice the news stories that typically grab your attention. What does your media diet consist of? What type of news stories do you always seem to gravitate to? For example, if you tend to always pay attention to corporate diversity and inclusion blunders, can you offer advice to corporate teams who are navigating culture shifts?

If you're a therapist who helps high achieving women work through the challenges of isolation, you may pay attention to news about women CEOs. If a high profile female CEO is in the news for alienating her male clients, could you write about the issues that may have led to her misconduct and the mindset one has to cultivate in order to successfully navigate a similar situation?

Use what you're reading and watching to prompt further exploration.

What conversations do you want to be a part of that don't already exist?

Sometimes there's a deafening silence around the issue that *you* want to debate. Mainstream media and your industry publications don't seem to know about it. They certainly don't acknowledge it in their coverage.

If the silence around a question, issue, or topic is driving you crazy, that's a sign you should be writing or speaking out about it. It may be something to build thought leadership around.

For example, when I pivoted from journalism to communications, it was right around the time that social media was becoming "a thing." Twitter was gaining traction and I became obsessed with how my former colleagues in the newsroom were using social media to find sources for their stories or even uncover breaking news.

I started writing about the topic and eventually launched a successful panel series featuring journalists from the Washington Post, NPR, CBS and others. I found my thought leadership pondering what was happening at the intersection of journalism, social media and public relations.

But it all started with my curiosity. I wanted to have a conversation that wasn't currently on the table.

Follow your curiosity. What conversation are you dying to have?

What questions have people asked?

This is perhaps the easiest place to start, especially for coaches and consultants. You likely have a long list of writing topics buried in your email inbox - they came to you in the form of questions, contact form entries, and LinkedIn direct messages. If you work in an office environment, you may have colleagues stop by your desk to pick your brain on your area of expertise. Have you considered that as a pathway to thought leadership?

As I always tell my clients - the world is telling you what they want from you in the form of the questions they're asking, so pay attention!

Here's an example from my own business. I offer free discovery sessions to get to know members of my audience and connect with potential new students for my academy. A great way for me to come up with new ideas for writing, social media and online programs is to simply look at the responses on my calendar form. Here's one entry I received:

Q: *What are your concerns about your brand? What specific project do you want to discuss?*

A: *My concerns are I don't understand how to package all that I am and do into one concise brand that anyone can understand. I have many humanitarian projects in the works, but need to go after more funding. I know that I cam not adequately branded to do this yet.*

This particular entry gave me not one but two great thought leadership content ideas!

I could write 'Multi-Passionate Professionals: How

to package all that you do into one concise brand,' or I could write '3 ways to properly position your nonprofit brand for massive funding.'

Voilà.

Like I said, you likely have an inbox full of thought leadership prompts - it's just up to you to uncover them.

You're also likely getting tons of verbal questions on your area of expertise. Start paying attention to the types of questions people are asking. Do you notice a theme?

Extracting thought leadership

Earlier in the book, you worked to create a clear brand statement, and establish your credibility. You should have a clear picture of what you've done, which gives your potential colleagues and customers the confidence that you can perform similarly for them. Now you're going to take what you've done, tease out the themes and create advice that you can use to help others while building your personal brand in the process.

Remember: you don't have to know everything, but if you're on a path and getting good results for your company, yourself, or your clients you likely have a great deal to teach. You can build your thought leadership and content around those teachings.

Finding your thought leadership

If you typically shy away from terms like "thought leader" or "expert" because you've yet to reach the top of your field, be encouraged that it is through sharing your ideas that you can position yourself as an expert and take yourself to the top of your industry.

Think about the people you admire in your field. They likely have written a book or given a talk that laid out their thought leadership. Think about your industry heroes: they likely have created content that changed your life, professionally at least. But before they sat down to write the book, author the paper, conduct the research, deliver the Ted Talk or edit the podcast, they were exactly where you are right now.

It's a process.

Take an inventory of your knowledge

Ask yourself the following questions:

- What do you know?
- What is your core message?
- What do people consistently thank you for?
- What questions are you always answering?
- What advice are you always giving freely to others?

You may have noticed that some of these questions appeared earlier in the book. You should be able to refer back to your responses when I asked them of you earlier. What themes emerge from your responses?

One way to drill a little deeper into this would be to think of the top three challenges you see the most from your colleagues, clients, or your stakeholders. What is their most common situation? What are they worried about the most? What do most people in their position need to know that they generally don't seem to know?

For example, in my coaching business the three challenges I see the most revolve around the question of clarity. People coming to me want to know:
- What is their expertise and unique genius?
- How do they build an audience, gain awareness, and grow their reach?
- How do they get people to buy what they're selling? How do they get clients or get promoted?

In my case, I have developed thought leadership content around all of these topics. If you take a look at my blog, you'll see content around this in addition to many of the other questions I am asked often.

Common points of frustration

What if people aren't directly asking you questions? In that case I encourage you to think back to those 'pull-your-hair-out' moments you have inevitably had when talking to colleagues, friends, or clients. Now to to be clear, I'm not referring to general moments of frustration, but instead I'm talking about when you're frustrated because you have a clear professional solution to your colleague's problem.

For example, back when my business was focused exclusively on social media, I found myself sitting in a coffeeshop one day with another public relations colleague. This colleague just couldn't grasp the concept of Twitter, which was rippling through our industry at the time. As we sipped our coffee, I found my frustration mounting because this person I cared about was dismissing a tool that could revolutionize her business. I wanted to pull out my hair in frustration and I couldn't get up from the table until she understood the power of the medium. I wanted to make sure she knew how to use it to connect with journalists and to amplify her own clients' messages.

I helped her set up her account and taught her the fundamentals of how to use the platform. She eventually got it and went from being a non-believer to an active user. She event went on to snag a popular social media conference as her client. Social media is a huge part of her current work as a publicist.

If I were to pull a piece of thought leadership content out of that example, it might look like one of the following:
- 'Why social media is a critical component of your communications work (my argument to her) or
- 'Five Steps to get started on Twitter' (a tactical piece of content that can help others).

Another moment of frustration, or "pull out my hair" moment for me was during a conversation with a childhood friend whom I'd been out of touch with for some time. As we were catching up, he told me how he was navigating in his career and how much his colleagues and supervisors relied on him to lead the conversations at social functions after work. Whenever the company hosted clients or important guests, he found himself making introductions and facilitating the flow of conversation. I immediately heard that as a point of genius and encouraged him to package it for his personal brand. Because he seemed so uncomfortable with the idea, and so lost as to where to start, it inspired me to write one of my most popular blog posts of all time - 'How to Turn Your Expertise into Income'.

Take a moment to reflect on your recent experiences. Is there something you know how to do so well that it bothers you when others can't do it? When did you see a friend or relative making a mistake that was simple for you to fix? When did you last encourage someone to make simple changes around your area of expertise?

Your prescription for change

At this point you've probably identified a topic and you're inspired to share content around a solution that can help people. But before you start creating, you have one more step to ensure your content is as impactful as possible. You'll need to take a little time to unpack your standard prescription for the problem you plan to address through your thought leadership content.

You have already heard me use the term "methodology" and you may have also heard the term "signature solution" or "signature methodology" as it relates to others in your field. Now this is not to be confused with the signatures we'll discuss later in the book. I've dedicated a whole chapter to that. Instead this signature solution is more of your prescription for change.

What is your signature solution?

A signature solution is your standard approach to solving the problem you most often see. Think of it as a doctor's prescription for the common cold, the remedy prescribed for influenza. The symptoms are so common, she sees them so much during cold and flu season that she can rattle the remedy off quickly. The same is true with you when you're operating in your gift. You likely don't even realize you're solving others' problems, and yet you are. If you need to, reflect back on those thank you moments: what preceded the expression of gratitude? What was your process to help the person you helped and solve the problem you solved?

Ask yourself, for your best work-related challenges and client experiences of the past, what was the most common recommendation you always made? If you're looking at your case studies, this would be paragraphs two and three. For your current work, in your opinion, what is the most effective and elegant way to solve the challenge at hand?

Once you know your prescription, you need to chart out your step by step process. In other words, what are the steps that comprise your signature solution? What is your methodology? In what order do these steps need to be completed?

My signature methodology

For example, many people ask me to help them build their personal brands. Since I started the personal branding coaching work as a pivot from public relations, I had a firm grasp of what people realistically needed to have in place in order to grab attention from the media or from the masses online. I knew that companies large and small struggled most with explaining their core mission or services in a clear way. So step one of my signature solution had to be centered around helping a new client achieve clarity and craft a clear message around that clarity. I made that step one of my process because it was the natural place I always started when working with clients. And without clarity around the message, I knew from experience that we wouldn't get far.

The second step in my signature solution was helping the client identify key pieces of evidence, then we'd look at opportunities to secure social proof before beginning the broadcasting phase.

So if you look at my product ***The Branding Box*** as an example of thought leadership, it is built around what I identified to be the 5 elements of personal brand positioning - the 5 steps of the personal brand process:
- create a clear, concise message
- gather evidence
- collect social proof
- develop thought leadership content
- broadcast your messages

From this example you can see how a signature solution can evolve from something as simple as a blog post.

Good content expands and contracts

Taking the example of The Branding Box further, you can see how something as simple as a blog post, i.e. 'How to use five elements of personal brand positioning to grow your audience' can evolve into something as involved as an information product. But it could also translate to a whole other medium like an event experience or conference. This is because good core content has the ability to expand or contract. By this I mean, the core elements of what you share could be summed up in an infographic, or taught over a series of three days conference style because there's so much meat to explore.

Another not-so-secret secret is this: once you have your core content idea down, you've also outlined a potential signature talk and a media interview.

I have shared the '5 elements of personal brand positioning' in almost every way possible. I've written about it, I continue to deliver webinars on it, I offer conference breakouts sessions and half-day bootcamps around it. For me, it is the core of my thought leadership and I continue to expand or contract it as I see fit. It is my prescription for change.

It's important to note that I was only able to identify the five elements after doing the process of inquiry we've been talking about all along. When I stopped and took a look at what it took me to get results from my best public relations initiatives, I was inspired to create a process that I could easily lead others through.

As you think about your signature solution and core content, don't make the mistake of simply copying what others are doing. Take the time to think about your process, how you do things, and what you have to add. Even if you believe whole-heartedly in another professional's methods, don't discount your own.

You may have a "secret sauce" or "special ingredient" that you unknowingly layer on top of the standard method. If you fail to adhere to the process of inquiry and solely build your content around what you've seen and read from others, you risk leaving out the very best part of what you uniquely have to offer.

A note for newly minted experts

Should you choose to take up the teacher-leader-expert mantle, you'll eventually exhaust what you know. You'll need to seek out new tools, new guidance, new research to gain a new understanding. The times may change and you may need to update, refresh, or reinvent. At that point, it's time to have a seat and learn what you need to learn to go to your next level.

On whichever end of the spectrum you fall, never be too afraid to from student to teacher, or too proud to go from teacher to student.

It's natural to evolve. Know when it's your time to step up and teach, or when it's your time sit down and learn.

Questions to Consider

- ❖ What do you know?
- ❖ What questions are you always answering?
- ❖ What advice do you always give freely to others?
- ❖ What is your signature solution?
- ❖ What is your step by step process to get results?
- ❖ What is your prescription for change?

7
HOW TO SHARE
DEVELOP A PERSONAL CONTENT STRATEGY

By now you've identified what you know and can share - your thought leadership expertise. But how can you now package that thought leadership into actual content for others to consume?

In this chapter we're going to break down the process of turning expertise into content.

From case study to content

Case studies are a great place to start from a content perspective because they can typically be published and shared as is. If it doesn't stand alone as its own article however, you can easily transform a case study into a piece of personal branding content that promotes your expertise.

Start with paragraph one and use the situation and the results as the title, for example: *'How one out of shape mom of two lost 20 pounds, reclaimed her health and went from stressed-out to zen in three months.'* This case study could be a great headline to showcase the work of a health and wellness coach.

Next, you'll want to generalize your advice and

pull out the 3-5 tips or steps that anyone could use. Remember the methodology concept we explored earlier? That will come into play here.

For example:
- First, take an inventory of your time, food intake and exercise
- Second, set three goals you can realistically accomplish in three months
- Third, decide on a lifestyle and wellness routine that will help you achieve these goals
- Then build time into your schedule to adhere to your routine
- Last, celebrate the first milestone

Obviously you'll take each of these steps and add some details about how to do each step correctly. You can add a story to bring it to life even more.

Or, you can opt to simply write the whole thing as a straight case study that showcases your thought process and approach to problem solving. Some industry publications like PRWeek publish case studies to inform their professional readership. Is there an industry publication that may be interested in sharing what's working in the industry from your perspective?

Other ways to package your content

In addition to case studies, here are a few popular ways to format thought leadership content that have worked really well for me and some of the experts I've supported. I've included the format as well as a few sample topics for each.

Ways and Reasons Lists
- 5 ways to reclaim your balance after trauma
- 4 ways to shake off the winter blues
- 5 reasons to build your brand in the New Year

Feature Lists
- 10 black women who are changing the faith community
- 5 best websites for women leaders
- 5 women of faith to follow on twitter (lists like these align you with other leaders AND and encourages featured influencers to share your work)

Common Mistakes

While mistakes may sound negative at first glance, they're a great way to build intrigue! For example:
- 7 ways you're keeping yourself from your calling
- 6 mistakes new business owners make
- 4 mistakes you're making with your digital communications strategy

Humans are naturally curious and headlines like these make readers want to investigate if they're making the mistakes on your list.

How to

Think about the questions people ask you about within your field of expertise. What advice do they commonly seek out from you?

Personal branding pro tip - if you don't already have one, you can make a list of your most frequently asked questions (FAQs) and generate introductory

content to answer those questions. Examples of how to articles:
- How to successfully hire your first employee
- How to develop your stakeholder engagement strategy
- How to get started with social media
- How to grow your audience from scratch

See?

Best Practices, Checklists and Trends
- New spring workouts you can do without a gym
- The 5 foods you need to incorporate into your summer diet to gain muscle and burn fat
- The FIRST three things you should do when you start your business
- 10 things you must do in the first 3 months of your marriage to secure your happily ever after

Profiles and Q & A Sessions
- Meico Whitlock shows burned out professionals how to achieve the ever elusive work-life balance
- Reisha Moxley shares tips for modern high achieving women working in male-dominated spaces
- A Q&A with media maven Arianna Huffington

Case Studies

Your case studies don't have to be related to **your** work results; you can create case studies after going behind the scenes with someone who has been successful in your industry, i.e.
- How a single mom built a multi-million dollar construction company from the ground up

- How a woman-owned construction company transformed an abandoned neighborhood into a thriving commercial district through community development.

By featuring case studies of others' success, you can also serve as a resource to your community by featuring other members of your industry - especially experts. In addition to your own thought leadership and ideas, you can feature the ideas of the leaders you admire (and align yourself with them, strategically). So if you have a podcast and you don't know what to say, but you find you're curious about other women and their stories, create interview opportunities.

This worked really well for me when I was a newbie in the public relations industry. Since I was dying to know about the day to day of different public relations professionals, I reached out to people I found interesting and requested an interview for my PR blog. This served to grow my personal brand, develop my content and build my network! I found that while it was tough to get important people on the phone with no just cause, I rarely heard no when I offered up an interview. Be strategic - by giving people exposure, you may be able to connect with people you've always wanted to meet. So don't be afraid to interview others especially if you're new in your business, as it's a great way to build awareness around yourself and align your name with your topic.

Other ways to package your genius

Your thought leadership can take many forms in

the digital age, and that's the exciting part about living in our current time. Once you've identified your knowledge, you can use it to share:

- a post on LinkedIn or your web site
- a guest article on a larger media site - or a magazine's web site
- a workshop or seminar
- a book
- a panel
- a conference
- a pre-recorded and edited video
- a live video
- a podcast episode
- an online course
- a coaching session
- a coaching program
- a special report
- an in-depth ebook
- an infographic

You get the idea!

I hope you can see from the examples I've shared that even if you're not a strong writer, you can still create content centered around your thought leadership ideas - you may just have to do it in a format like audio or video that works better for you.

But whatever format feels best to you, I always advise people to try to start with written thought leadership content. The reason to write is this - when people are searching for a solution to their problem, there's a greater chance that they'll stumble across your work online if you've written an article or published something around it.

Written articles are also a great way to embed keywords to help with search engine optimization - SEO - for your personal brand. Dozens of clients have found me online due to the articles I've written that have added to my digital footprint, helping me rank for search terms like "personal branding coach" or "personal brand consultant."

What keywords and terms would you like your personal brand to rank highly for?

Keep this in mind even as you develop video or audio content: the words you use to title any piece of content - whether a podcast episode or YouTube video - can help or hurt your chances to be found online.

Mistakes that keep your content from gaining traction

When I started writing as a print reporter for a newspaper in Washington, DC I knew I was a strong writer. I was a former English major and had been writing for most of my life, so I was fairly confident in my ability to share my ideas through words.

But what I didn't know was how being a strong writer isn't enough if you want your content to gain traction.

As I learned the business of news, I quickly found out that subject-verb agreement and flowery prose were just the beginning.

I had to learn how to pitch a concept to editors before they'd green light the story. I had to craft the perfect headline to intrigue new readers. And I had to go deep into one area if I wanted to brand myself and own my own "beat" - journalism parlance for the topic you write about most authoritatively and readers know you for.

The same goes for you.

You have to know how to sell your ideas if you ever want people to find and consume them, and that starts with branding yourself as a credible source of information on your topic.

Here are 5 principles you must keep in mind if you want to get traction through your thought leadership content. Keep in mind, I've used these principles to gain traction in several different focus areas, and have helped hundreds of clients do the same.

Principle 1
Establish a clear focus

If you're not getting traction or leads from your content, you may be talking about too many things. As a result, people don't know what you do, what they can rely on you for, or why they should be reading (or watching or listening to) what you're putting out there.

You may be like the many people I see who want to tackle too many topics when they first start out. This can easily confuse your audience and cause them to tune out before they've even given you a chance.

Focus on one topic and build traction with that topic before introducing new topics of expertise to your audience.

Principle 2
Create content from a strategic position

Before you publish a LinkedIn post, a Medium article or even a tweet, have you thought about what you want your audience to do as a result of experiencing your content?

For example, if you record a podcast about positioning yourself for a career pivot, are you using the episode to introduce your career pivoting workshop, tease one of the points in your upcoming career pivoting book, or connect your readers to your online community of career pivot-ers?

When you fail to invoke a strategy - even loosely - you can easily fall into the trap of creating content just to create it. You then end up with a ton of content that goes nowhere.

Ultimately, the goal of your content should be not only to position you as an expert but to also connect you to what you want more of - more job interviews, more speaking engagements, more book sales, more social media followers or more coaching clients.

Before you start creating content, think about what you want more of, and what the next steps could be for getting there. How is each piece of your content helping your audience take the next step?

Principle 3
Position your content as a solution

Sometimes, during the personal branding process we make the mistake of thinking that our content should be only about, well, *ourselves*.

However, if you want people to read, watch, listen to, engage with and share your work it ultimately has to somehow be a solution to a problem they have.

Now this doesn't mean you can only write "how to" articles or shoot informational videos tied to your expertise - your content can also be a solution when it makes someone laugh, inspires them to move forward, gets them out of a rut, or sparks a creative idea.

Before you create your next piece of content, think about your intention behind your solution. Are you setting out to inform, educate, entertain, or inspire?

Principle 4
Make your content easy to find online

When I work with personal branding clients, my goal is to help them to stand out beyond the people they *already* know.

But what I see most often when giving content feedback are bad headlines - the titles of the videos, blog posts Medium articles or podcast episodes - are too specific to attract an audience of strangers.

One thing I learned early when I was working as a print reporter in the newsroom is how important headlines are to the publishing process. You need to quickly capture the attention and intrigue of your audience so they want to keep going with you. If your headline only makes sense to you and people who know you, two critical issues emerge.

For one, if your headline includes a reference that is too personal, most people won't know what it means so they won't be intrigued enough to click. Secondly, without a good headline, it will be difficult for your content to pop up in a general internet search.

Before you press publish, ask yourself "would anyone Google this headline when searching for information on this topic?"

Principle 5
Be consistent in the beginning

Even if you feel like a broken record, you have to talk about the same topic over and over again and offer value consistently in order to build trust. Only when you build trust can you build an audience of engaged followers who will keep coming back to you.

The dynamic between creators and their audience is a relationship like any other, so you can't expect overnight intimacy.

Think about the people you have full faith and trust in. They may be trusted friends, confidantes, employees, or spiritual gurus. Before blindly handing over your complete trust in them, they had to prove themselves to you, right? Trust didn't happen overnight.

The same goes for you and your audience. You have to keep showing up consistently, especially in the beginning when you're working on gaining traction.

Don't expect raving fans overnight. Hang in there with your audience and consistently add value around your topic of expertise so they have the chance to begin to see you as their guru on your chosen topic.

Questions to consider

- What is one topic that you can build thought leadership around?
- Who can you list and engage?
- What formats will you use? Audio? Video? Writing?
- How can you be more strategic before you create ?
- What goals will your content help you accomplish?
- What topics are you motivated to speak about?
- What topic could illustrate your passion and expertise today?
- What current events or industry news can you comment on?
- Brainstorm 3-5 topics you can write 750 words on. Where will you submit for publication?

8
IDEAS TO INCOME
MONETIZE YOUR BRAND THROUGH SIGNATURES

What's the difference between an expert, and an expert who gets paid?

Packaging.

And by packaging, I don't mean a beautiful logo or fancy website. I simply mean this: the experts you see making six and seven figures from what they know (even if their knowledge isn't all that great) all have one thing in common: they've successfully packaged their expertise into a product that allows them to transfer what they know to others, for a fee.

That's what a signature product or service allows you to do. And this is typically the very first thing I help new clients think through when we work together.

What about you? How can you package what you know in a way that others can purchase it?

Now before I get too deep into this chapter, if you're not ready to position your brand for money-making opportunities just yet, feel free to skip this chapter. You may be building your brand for visibility so you can get a promotion or land a new role. That's totally fine!

Just know that if you choose to monetize in the future (which I think is a smart target to keep in mind for everyone - whether you have a full-time job or own your business) this chapter lays out how you can begin to do that in a way that works for you.

For those of you who are ready to turn your personal brand into revenue, let's do this!

You can package it NOW

There are so many ways to package your genius. But for whatever reason, most people seem to think that packaging what they know is something they can't do today - they need to wait until a future magical time when they'll be "ready". Or they think their genius isn't good enough yet. Or they think they need to spend thousands of dollars on a website or fancy graphics that will make people want to buy.

But let me let you in a little secret - you don't have to wait - can package and sell your expertise today. Because there is someone who needs what you know, just the way it is right now.

I am willing to bet that if you are reading this, you have something you can package to sell. You just have to figure out what that is and how you should format it. To get your wheels turning, I thought I'd share some ideas.

Ways to package your genius to sell

1. Book or Ebook
2. Online Video Course
3. Webinar
4. Master Class
5. Networking Reception
6. Signature Luncheon
7. 3 Day Conference
8. 1 Day Summit
9. Boxed Information Product
10. Corporate Bootcamp
11. One-on-One Signature Coaching Session
12. Group Coaching or Strategy Session
13. 6-Month Group Coaching Mastermind
14. 2-Day Small Group Retreat
15. Audio Series
16. Workbook + Audio Download
17. Sponsored Dinner Party
18. 3-Month Consulting Package
19. 90 Minute Brainstorming or Strategy Session
20. Document/Website/Product Review
21. Keynote Speech
22. Conference Breakout Session
23. Online Office Hours
24. Paid Membership Community
25. Subscription Box
26. Monthly Q + A Call
27. Ticketed Networking Lunch with Speaker
28. Half-Day Ticketed Seminar
29. Excursion Experience + Coaching

30. Networking Brunch
31. Video Series (Boxed set or hosted online)

This is just the tip of the iceberg. As you can see, there are endless ways to package your genius to sell. And the beauty of it is, you only need one format to start creating revenue for yourself today. So which format will you start with?

Signature offers

While there are many ways to monetize your personal brand, I'm going to focus on signature offers.

First of all, what do I mean by a signature offer? I'm defining a signature offer as a revenue-generating program that requires specialized marketing and aligns with your personal or business brand. It is a service, event, product or program that becomes a calling card for you: when people think of you, they think of your signature.

One powerful and profitable strategy for building your personal brand is by developing a breakout event, program or service both you and your clients will love. You're going to uncover something new that you can package and add to your current business mix. But this won't be just any old offer; it will be one that is inspired, reflective of your gifts, one that adds tremendous value to your customers and brings you utter joy! For those of you who think it's too soon to talk signatures because you don't have any clients yet, pay attention to this chapter.

No matter where you are in your business or brand, you can effectively develop a new signature and create something that will help you do the work of promoting yourself and your business while bringing in revenue of some sort *at the same time*.

As you know from reading this far, I believe you should look for clues that indicate what's **already** working for your personal brand and build from there. Can you duplicate a past success? Can you create success around an area where you've already shown some degree of promise?

If you stop to think about where you are right now, what has been working? What work are you doing - and perhaps not getting paid for - that you could potentially turn into a signature offer? What are some of the clues you may be overlooking?

Everyone is in a different place – there's no right or wrong starting point. This process has worked for clients making less than fifty thousand dollars to clients making over ten million. Even if you are trying to figure out your next move, or how to pivot, you can grow your brand (or the new direction of your brand) around a new signature offer.

First things first, let's get focused. As you read the rest of the chapter, I want you to focus your mental energy on creating only one thing that can re-energize your brand and put you on the map. Especially if this is your first time creating any type of signature offer, I want you to focus your energy on an offer that falls into one of the following three categories: a signature live event, a signature consulting or coaching session or a signature online class. As you can see on the table below, you can start simply in phase one and build from there with the phase two and phase three examples. Use the table as a guide for how your signature could evolve over time.

Phase One	Phase Two	Phase Three
a live event (2-3 hours, i.e. panel or networking reception)	a social or educational event series	a 1-3 day conference
a signature consulting or coaching session (1-2 hours)	a signature coaching or consulting package of multiple sessions	a longterm program engagement of 6+ months
a signature online webinar or Masterclass (1-2 hours)	a signature course or training program (4 weeks+)	a group Mastermind or Membership (one year)

Second, understand that developing a signature is actually **a personal branding strategy in and of itself,** not just a way to monetize what you know. Money is not the only benefit of developing a signature offer.

Each signature offer I've created for my business has brought more than additional revenue. Each one also added hundreds of names to my email list, generated brand recognition, and attracted media attention as well as invitations to speak. My live events helped position me in a crowded communications market and helped me reach industry influencers when I was not yet one.

So understand that what you're about to read can have multiple outcomes for your personal brand.

My signature(s) story

One of the reasons I'm such a champion of brand signatures is because I've used them to help me reinvent myself and my business multiple times. I have used signatures to go from an industry unknown to an industry influencer, and I've helped others do the same.

Twitter + Pitch = *Twitch!*

My very first signature was a live panel event that I evolved into an event series I held over the course of three years. After having been out of the newsroom for a few years, I started to notice how much social media was beginning to take over communications.

As a former journalist, I wondered how journalists were now using social media to communicate with sources and find news. At the urging of a few friends, I organized a panel event that convened media professionals from the Washington,

DC area. Using the hashtag #twitchdc, we had a powerful conversation about how media was changing.

The event worked because it was something my audience of communications professionals found interesting. It also engaged influencers - in this case reporters - those communications professionals wanted desperately to meet.

The event essentially "put me on the map" in the Washington communications space. But it didn't only work for me. I've coached others to use this same strategy to establish themselves in a new industry or a new geographic market.

The 90 minute brand brainstorm

One of my favorite and likely most profitable signatures to date was my one-off strategic coaching and consulting session - the 90 Minute Brand Brainstorm. I launched the session as a signature offer after becoming hearing from clients who were in need of social media and marketing ideas for their careers or small businesses. I essentially formalized a process to allow people to "pick my brain" for a fee. I started out selling this service for $249 and quickly found myself selling 3-6 sessions each week.

While the sessions brought in additional revenue to augment my PR business, their greatest value lied in the brand recognition I gained from having a calling card. The session was successful because I focused exclusively on marketing it for about one year. During that time, it was the only thing I talked about. I had custom graphics developed for it and marketed it singularly and aggressively on social media.

The Branding Box

My signature product The Branding Box was an outgrowth of the 90 minute sessions I'd done with individual clients. I looked at most common problems of clients and developed a base personal branding curriculum to address that set of common problems. Once the Branding Box was established, it became the core curriculum for my company, and the starting point for all personal branding work.

The Branding Box did really well because it was different. In the age of online courses, a physical box was different enough to stand out. Now, I don't claim that this box was the first packaged information product to ever be created. But because most information products had shifted to digital, an analog solution stood out.

The box was my first experience creating a scalable offer that didn't require my time or energy. People bought it, my team and I shipped it, and the client could have their experience without any additional input from me. It added six figures to my annual revenues in its first two years.

Package Your Genius Academy

At a certain point, I craved community among my clients and followers. I wanted to connect more deeply with people who were experiencing the branding box, and I wanted a way to connect with my clients in a group. The academy is a group coaching program and that built on the content in the Branding Box.

As you may be able to see, each of these signatures came out of an existing need my clients had, or a desire I had personally. What are your customers already telling you? What questions are *begging* to be answered? What conversations would you like to be a part of?

Your signature style

As you approach creating a signature, look at what is already working for yourself. What's your style? When are you at your best? How could you easily add to something you're already doing? The key word is easily. Bonus points if you can package what you're already doing and put a price on it.

I see so many people who try to fit themselves into an idea of the business or profession they're in. PR people for example – on the surface it's a very social business, but there are a number of introverts who are great at it. You may not do event planning and instead want to do media strategy.

The beauty of creating a signature is that since it is going to be tailored to your style, it can be anything that you want it to be. You can and should build fun into your signature. And if you build it in a way that feels right to you, you'll get better results for your clients or customers.

Your signature is a solution

First, remember the problem you solve - your

signature should essentially be a more in-depth example of a signature solution. People are less likely to buy in if your signature isn't solving an immediate problem, so first ask yourself what problem your signature will solve. When approaching your signature as a solution, remember some of those questions we asked earlier in the book:

- What problems do you currently solve?
- What problems would you like to solve - you want to work on this but you haven't yet made the time?
- What do people keep asking you to solve but you haven't?
- What would be the results of your solution?
- What audience has the problem you solve?
- Who is your tribe – where are you already influential? Where do you already know lots of people. Where are you trusted?
- Who is attracted to you – it may be a new audience – someone you haven't thought about
- Who usually raises their hand to work with you already?

I gave you a ton of ideas of formats so maybe when it's time for your to write your book or package your genius some other way you can come back to those ideas and brainstorm. But for this chapter, remember I want you to focus on either an event, a coaching session or a training program.

Live events

Live events could fall into a few categories: socializing, networking, coaching and training. Which type of experience do you want to have? Remember, we will start with one event, in its most elemental form and grow from there.

For example, if you want to host a conference, try to successfully host a workshop or networking event first to determine who your audience is and how much your audience responds.

Live event ideas:
- an annual 1-3 day conference
- workshop or mini-retreat
- weekend retreat
- networking event – luncheon, brunch, or sit down dinner with a featured speaker
- sponsored happy hour or reception
- sit down dinners

Consulting and coaching sessions

I love one on one coaching or consulting session because they are a great way to build your brand and develop your track record around your topic when you're starting something new and you don't have the social proof that you need to market it. Eventually, if you're doing it right, you'll start getting referrals. If you haven't done anything start with a session. It's the easiest way to start selling your expertise!

Even if you're not a certified life coach or leadership coach, you can sell your strategic ideas, expertise and accountability to others. You're probably already giving people advice and letting people pick your brain, so get your feet wet by offering a paid 30 minute session, 60 minute session, or 90 minute session. This is one of my favorite formats because it takes what you're already doing and monetizes it.

Once you've successfully done sessions or are really confident with what solution your 1:1 will get may be time to create a longer solution like a 6-week program where you talk with the client weekly, or a 30 day challenge with online support. For a coaching package, you want to think back to your prescription. What do people need to get the best result from working with you? Do they need to talk to you for an hour each week? How much interaction and what interaction do you want to give them? Monetize these by the amount you want to make per hour OR a packaged price that is based on the value this solution will eventually add.

Training program

An online or in-person training program is great for corporate clients - pricier, 1 day; corporate training programs go for a lot more if you build in training over the course of several months or a full year. So if you develop an employee training program for example you can sell that to a corporation.

Online training

You can also create a one-off signature training and deliver it via webinar. Don't sleep on webinars because like coaching or strategy sessions they are also an easy place to start.

The difference is, webinars are an exampled of a leveraged income stream because you have the opportunity to share and potentially share your expertise with a group of people instead of one individual client. You can make much more money with the same amount of effort when you leverage your time and expertise this way.

Years ago when I first started toying with webinars as something to sell, I was surprised that I was able to get 50 people to sign up for a webinar I charged $50. In roughly 90 minutes, I made $2500 from teaching a class that didn't even feel like work to teach. I was hooked!

I have done other paid webinars, and charged much more for them, and I can't say there are many drawbacks to sharing your knowledge this way. The community you foster through group teaching and the amount of money you can bring in from teaching groups vs. individuals is unparalleled.

Online or masterminds are also great if you want to create your information one time, leverage it for groups, and resell it again and again. My online mastermind Package Your Genius Academy has been a great way to teach a set of lessons to a group. I love the format.

Pricing your signature

When it's finally time to price your solution, ask yourself how will your signature be positioned in the market? What are other similar offers going for? Do you want to be above or below that? How do you want to be perceived – accessible or as a luxury service? Do some research on how your competitors are pricing their similar offers and look for precedence. Don't reinvent the wheel!

Also, think about how your signature will be positioned within your business in relation to the other things you offer. For example, after I introduced the Branding Box, all of my 1:1 services had to go up in price as the box became the baseline. If my information product cost $500, working with me one on one had to cost at least 2-3x that in order to make sense in the universe of my offerings. So where does your signature fit in your matrix of your other offers? Is this an entry level service? Or is this for your VIPs?

For example – my group masterminds are priced lower than private strategy days because they are a group offer and meant to be an introductory service.

Consider how much time delivering your signature will take and how much your time is worth to you. What will make you feel duly compensated? Once you figure in the assessment, the meeting and follow up if it's coaching, the research and preparation time, travel time and delivery if it's speaking or training – how many hours will you have to sink into the product before you feel good about delivering it to the customer? And how much is each hour of that time worth to you?

Lastly, consider what feels good. My intuitive approach is to think about a time in the past when I offered a solution for free. After it took longer than you thought it would, and all kinds of issues popped up. What would have made you feel fairly compensated? If you're not offering these services full time, make sure you are not too conservative. Could you meet your full-time revenue goals and pay your operating expenses and taxes if you were selling this signature full-time?

Do's and Don'ts

I know this sounds like a lot, but try not to get overwhelmed! Just breathe, and use the questions at the end of the chapter to capture your thoughts and create your plan of action.

Don't make the mistake of thinking that creating a signature is something you have to do later. Profiting from a signature offer doesn't have to take very long.

Several years ago, I had a client who came to me about how to grow her public affairs consultancy. During our conversation she let it slip that she really had a passion for empowering young women. On the spot, we were able to ideate a new event series. She secured a speaker and hosted her first event 3 weeks after that conversation. It was so well-received that she made it a series and has since done 5 or 6 other events and expanded to her second city.

Think about that: from event concept to sold out event in three weeks. What could that mean for you? Remember: things can grow if you are willing to put your energy and focus behind them and let go of your own limiting beliefs about what is possible. Let go of your excuses that may come up later when it's time to put this into practice.

Questions to consider

- What topic or topics could you build a signature offer around?
- Do you have a solid piece of instructional content that could potentially be expanded into a larger paid offering? For example, a 7 step blog post that could be expanded into a book?
- Do you have a speaking presentation deck that could be repurposed into a webinar, MasterClass or online course?
- What network of people could you bring together for a live event? Around what topic?
- What featured speakers would you like to see? Who in your network would other people pay to see?
- What's your style? What is the most comfortable way for you to deliver your best results?
- Which formats would you like to try?
- When can you realistically introduce your first new signature to your current audience?

9

PIVOT

REROUTE YOUR PATH WHEN THE TIME COMES

What happens when the career path you originally set out on doesn't take you where you want to go? What happens when the business you spent so much time bringing to stops bringing you fulfillment? You take stock of your skills, assess what's working, identify a new course and pivot.

One year after I finally mustered the courage to go all in on my coaching business, I found out that I'd won an award as the life and business coach of the year.

Winning the award made me reflect because truthfully, I was an "accidental coach". Recall that I had a background in journalism and communications, and had made a name for myself in the communications field. I was so scared to label myself a coach because I thought it would erase all of the hard work I'd done up to that point to position myself as a credible professional in the public relations and communications field. Yet I couldn't deny the market demand.

I was always the one in my circle offering some type advice (you should be using Twitter to connect with your customers!), encouragement (you know you're really good at this...why don't you make this a business?) and tweaks (add your website URL to your email signature!) to colleagues and friends.

Only after being urged on by a good friend did I start offering brainstorming sessions to people in need of marketing and PR help. But I was surprised to find that my brand of coaching would veer beyond marketing tactics and social media strategies. I was just doing what came naturally to me. I was helping people see who they really were so that they could then become the people they always suspected they could be.

But if you'd have told me that I would win awards for coaching, I would not have believed you. I was speaking, blogging, and working in nonprofit and small business PR. From my perspective, I thought the PR industry was the be-all, end-all for me. And I was happy with that - I loved the industry. But the thing about remaining open to possibility is, you don't know where you will end up next!

As a high achieving professional, you have likely spent a lot of time getting trained to do what you do. You have invested so much time and money into becoming who you are, to making a name for yourself or reaching a certain income threshold that it may feel like a lot to give up.

But even if you haven't considered pivoting, there are so many opportunities to use your skills in a different way. And it's easier than ever before to connect with the audience who needs those skills.

People, tasks or impact?

When you're ready to pivot, first you want to do a self inventory and take stock of your brand assets. What do you have to offer a new audience or work environment? Where have you felt excited at work in the past? What audiences do you enjoy working with?

Sometimes your career pivot may not be a complete 180 - you may just need to change one aspect of how you're doing what you do in order to see a marked difference in your experience. For example, you may be an attorney who loves the law but you're currently miserable because you're not practicing the type of law that makes the most sense for your skills.

What would happen if you changed your industry, say from corporate law to non-profit advocacy law, or from government to self employed legal professional? You may initially think you need to leave the legal profession completely, when a slight shift would make all the difference in the world.

Similarly, a shift in audience could be just what you need. Most people get a bigger sense of fulfillment when they're able to make an impact on an audience that matters to them. So while you may be a communications professional currently using your skills to amplify the messages of a major beauty brand, you may be drawn to women-owned small businesses who could see a much greater impact from your talents. While it may be nice to work with a big name brand, your personality may be better suited to a more intimate, startup work environment where everyone's efforts are felt tenfold.

This is key.

Often times I speak with clients who are tempted to throw away their entire work history when a slight shift is all that's really required. When you think about the aspects of your work that drain you, are they centered around the people, the tasks or the impact?

Think through the common threads that have defined your best days. What projects did you look forward to in the past? What type of work were you doing? What tasks were involved? What audience did you serve? That can give you insights into what you want to do.

Then research, read, absorb all of the information you can find about your potential new field(s). Try to find someone else who is already living your best life at work - read about them and how they got started, how they got their big break.

Study their path and take the best lessons for yourself.

Revisit the archives

While the high achiever in you may push you to constantly create new things and top your old ideas, at some point it's okay to go back to the archives, literally and figuratively. Because even if something didn't work in the past, you may have the resources, knowledge, skills and network to make it work now.

You don't always have to create something brand new to create something of value. If you've been creating value for others for any length of time, there is likely plenty of value in what you've already done and said, and there are plenty of people who've not discovered your work yet. Instead of fixating on a new tactic, project or idea or convincing yourself that everyone already knows what you've known for a long time, ask yourself if maybe it's time to revisit a good idea whose time may have finally come.

Chances are, if you showed an aptitude for something early in your life, you got pushed into that direction so you could tangible benefits of doing the thing that perhaps didn't come so easily for others.

But there was probably something else you longed to do or try, even if you didn't have the vocabulary to articulate that longing.

And since you were smarter or more athletic or better at math than those around you, you let someone else - usually a very well-meaning someone - tell you how you should make use of your talents, instead of exploring the possibilities yourself.

A degree (or two or three) later, and you may find yourself as a very successful person in your field but perhaps you feel creatively bankrupt. Whatever the case may be, that longing is still there. And it's growing louder.

Guess what? We are complex beings who may

excel at several different things. Your aptitude in one area doesn't always mean that it's the path you should stay on forever. And while you may have had wild success in a field, that doesn't mean you've used up your 'success tokens' in this life. You may have 1, 5, 10 or even more reinventions and countless success stories left in the potential you haven't yet had the courage to explore - if you only give yourself a chance.

You never know where you are meant to make a difference.

You may be on an incredible career or entrepreneurial path next year that you aren't even aware of today. So if you haven't found your lane in life, business or even love, haven't found success in the lane that you thought you were meant to be in, don't be discouraged. When you are brave enough to venture down a path not knowing where it will lead - when you have the courage to, in essence, follow your heart - things can change in an instant.

Doing something completely new

If you should decide you want to do something completely new and you need a fast way to break into your new area of expertise, refer back to chapter 8 on brand signatures.

A pivot is not the time to be subtle - you must be aggressive in how you talk about what you do, the type of content you share and the type of people you align yourself with.

In my opinion, a brand pivot is the one time

when it's acceptable to be obnoxious in telling people what you're about.

Think about it: we become known for what we do repeatedly. So it stands to reason that if we repeatedly share information on a certain topic, we'll eventually align ourselves with that topic. If we are repeatedly seen with certain people, others will begin to think of us in relation to our associates. If we are

Questions to consider

- ❖ What path have you always wanted to explore but haven't yet had the courage to?
- ❖ What do people often ask for your support around?
- ❖ What service do others request for you that you don't currently offer?
- ❖ If you could try anything right now and be guaranteed a success, what would that thing be?
- ❖ If you're currently unfulfilled on your path, do you want to change your industry, tasks or your impact?
- ❖ What is one small change you can make to test the waters of a new direction?

STEP 4
MAKE YOURSELF VISIBLE

Everyday, I see crazy-talented people who are flying under the radar. Because of their lack of visibility, the damage is two-fold: talented individuals are not making the money or making the impact they could. And, the people who could benefit most from those talents are left in the dark.

If you're like many people I talk to, you may feel frustrated because although you do great work, you don't have the exposure and platform you'd like. You may have been raised professionally on the idea that doing good work would be the key to your career advancement. But unfortunately, doing great work is not enough anymore. To get to where you're trying to go, you need to shine a spotlight on your skills, expertise and achievements. You need to let more people know about you.

Tell me if any of these scenarios sound familiar:

Your bio doesn't reflect the magic of who you are.

You've only half-heartedly tackled your social media presence because you're not sure how you should approach it.

Your message is unclear - your words fall flat and don't connect with your target audience.

People you work with rave about you, but your public platform is limited to the people you come in contact with on a day-to-day basis. You're essentially the best kept secret in your corner of the marketplace.

You crave a bigger platform. You want to speak on stages and get covered in the press, but have no idea where to even start.

To put it succinctly, you have a BIG vision for yourself and your talents, as you should. But you're not quite sure how to realize it.

You're on step four of five in this sequence. If you've been wondering where all this introspective work was going, in the following chapters, you'll learn how to amplify the message you've worked so hard to clarify.

10
TAP INTO SOCIAL MEDIA
LEVERAGE ONLINE TOOLS AND YOUR DIGITAL PRESENCE

This is not a book on social media, as there have been hundreds of books written on that topic alone. Furthermore, it's my hope that this book will survive the test of time. Perhaps fifty years from now, social media won't exist and will have been replaced by telepathy, or the next wave of communication. So to me, the tools are relevant for today, but the most important thing to know is *how and what to communicate*, whatever the medium.

As for which social media platforms to hop on, it really depends on what you do. For most professionals, service-based business owners or knowledge workers, LinkedIn, Facebook and Twitter are three solid platforms. Add Instagram if what you offer is visual and the most current video streaming social network if you like to chat and you're good on camera.

For experts, I recommend that you commit to at

least three social media platforms and try to develop a habit of posting regularly. If you have no digital presence whatsoever, start with one platform and focus on it exclusively until you have traction.

The following ideas are a buffet for you to pick and choose from, and show you a thought process to use when approaching social media. But by all means, don't dare feel overwhelmed or like you have to do everything on the list!

LinkedIn

As we watch social media mature, LinkedIn stands out as a network that can only grow in relevance. In 2017, the social network had 467 million users around the world. It was the largest professional social networking platform and offers an unmatched opportunity to connect with professionals around the globe.

I have personally used LinkedIn to grow my business beyond the boundaries of my city and even country. I have used LinkedIn to connect with - and land clients from Berlin, Saudi Arabia, the United Kingdom, South Africa, and Toronto in addition to Detroit, Cincinnati, and New York City.

The real opportunities I see for personal branding relate back to the SEO possibilities I mentioned earlier. For most LinkedIn users, a web search for their name will produce their LinkedIn profile as one of the top search results. For many of you, your LinkedIn profile is the very first search result that comes up when searching for your name!

Look at it this way: if someone is considering you for a job opportunity, media opportunity, or business opportunity, they are most certainly going to do a search for your name first. Since LinkedIn is most likely to show up on page one of that search you have an easy way to make a first impression with your profile. Beyond updating your summary with an engaging bio and adding a catchy headline, here are a few ways you can engage on LinkedIn:
- use the status **updates** to share what you're up to
- write longer **posts** to display thought leadership
- join or START an industry focused group to connect with people in your industry, network with influencers, connect members of your tribe, or connect with your customers.

Twitter

I've engaged on Twitter since the early days and it shows no signs of slowing down. In fact, as more industries understand the medium, they are using it as a second web search when looking for information about people.

For example, I reached out to a television producer colleague of mine to share information about a public relations client who had a great health story to share. My media friend listened to my pitch, before heading straight to Twitter to look up my client. She wanted to get a feel for my client's "thoughts in real time" since the show would require a hard-hitting interview. She was disappointed not to find more engagements on my client's Twitter and informed me that she had to "sell" the interview to her senior producers, and a part of the due diligence they would inevitably do involved researching her tweets.

That conversation was a wake-up call to me as a personal branding advisor. I now encourage all clients who are seeking to book coveted national media interviews to not only share content online, but also react to any breaking news in their industry. As spots get more and more competitive, producers are evaluating you everywhere. What are you putting out there?

Overall, the most common thing I hear from people who don't want to engage on Twitter is *"I don't get it. I don't understand how to use it, so I don't…"*

While I would typically encourage you to go with what feels right, in the case of personal branding, you may not be able to ignore it. If you're an author looking for a traditional book deal, or an expert looking for media opportunities, the people who have the power to hire you will look at your Twitter to get a sense of your "platform".

Here are a few ideas for engagement on Twitter:
- share your past articles again to help those pieces get more exposure
- engage with influencers by retweeting their updates and talking to them directly
- tweet using keywords on industry hashtags
- share your original articles and guest posts
- start a thread to tweet your advice in a series of

updates
- humanize yourself by showing your personality, humor and wit
- join Twitter chats to grow your following
- start your own Twitter chat to brand yourself around an issue or topic
- share updates in real time from events and conferences to connect with fellow attendees

Facebook and Instagram

Facebook has come under fire in recent years for its bait and switch practices. I can recall investing consistently over a period of months to grow the audience of one of my business pages, only for Facebook to change its algorithm so that those very fans I'd attracted were no longer able to see my updates unless I paid to "boost" posts from my page. That was frustrating for sure, but even in spite of that, I still see Facebook as a huge opportunity for small businesses and personal brands.

I remember what it was like to do *business* before the era of social media. I remember having to network religiously, and attend conferences in other states just to raise my profile beyond my personal network. And while I still network and travel to conferences, I can't ignore how much easier tools like Facebook have made it to grab the attention of someone across town or across the globe. So for as long as I can afford to participate, I will. I see the platform as a privilege for small business owners. I don't put all of my marketing eggs in its basket for sure, but since it boasts 2 billion users, it's definitely the biggest social marketplace to be in.

Whether you're just starting out on Facebook or you want to re-engage your existing presence, here are some ways to build community and tend to your tribe using Facebook:

- use private groups to build your tribe by giving group members early access to updates and product information
- use groups and pages to share new content such as blog posts, podcasts, and your media interviews
- share snippets of your upcoming book to generate prior interest and pre-sell copies
- preview speakers at your event to create anticipation and sell event tickets
- go live with video to share your advice, share a quick thought, remind your audience about something that's coming up, or even to tell them to read/listen to/watch a new piece of content
- share memes and tips visually

Instagram

- show snippets of your personality
- show behind the scenes in your business and lifestyle to humanize yourself and your company
- visually show "how to" content through branded graphics

All - create a signature hashtag that you can use to unify your posts, a la #packageyourgenius.

Three kinds of tools

While technology is ever evolving, I've found there are three categories of tools you can lean on to help you keep up with social media tasks: scheduling and automation, engagement and design.

Scheduling and automation

Many top social media influencers don't attempt to post their social media updates in real time. Instead, they use automation tools to help them. Whether you use Edgar, Hootsuite, Buffer, or a new tool that has come on the market, find a social media scheduling tool that will allow you to pre-load content to be shared on the schedule of your choosing.

Engagement

Automated engagement tools have received mixed reviews and I'm personally not a fan of them. However, for the right business they can work as well as scheduling. Automated engagement tools will automatically "like," "tweet," or "comment," on a post that meets a pre-determined range of criteria. For example, if I wanted to stay on top of new posts under the hashtag #packageyourgenius, I could set up an automation tool to "like" every new post that uses that hashtag. This is as risky as it sounds, though. Since you can't predict exactly what people will be using your hashtag for, you can't predict what your account will "like." I've found it works best for me to steer clear of automated engagement, but I see how it could be helpful for someone who wants to send a welcome tweet to every new customer to acknowledge a purchase, or further engage with visitors to a brick and mortar establishment.

Design

Social media has become increasingly visual so it is in your best interest to make your social media posts as visually appealing as possible. Design is no longer only the domain of designers - anyone with a smartphone can download apps like Wordswag to spruce up social media images. Free online design sites like Canva have replaced professional design programs like Adobe PhotoShop for many.

A social media plan

If you don't have time to publish your content by hand, lean on these automation tools. Use the scheduling tools - don't be shy! Start with one platform that you can master.

For LinkedIn, a status update 1-2x/week is good and a weekly post would be considered aggressive.

For Twitter, you have to feed the beast. I'd recommend at least two tweets per day, but 6-8 is more ideal if you want to gain traction with your personal brand. Those posts would need to be a mix of sharing

On Instagram I try to post one photo daily, but some business owners are more aggressive and post up to 12 times each day. It depends on your personal brand and the audience you want to attract. If your potential customers and clients are hanging out on Instagram, by all means, post away.

For Facebook, depending on how you use it, or

what you're using (Page vs. Group) you can post on your page 3-4x/week but you need to engage in groups daily. So remember what is expected for each platform and factor that into your time.

Live streaming via video depends on how much bandwidth you have for video but those who love it tend to broadcast daily. If you plan to do it, a weekly live broadcast is a good goal to shoot for.

Set some social media goals

When my goal was to grow Instagram, I signed up for an engagement automation tool to help me with the engagement once I discovered that to grow your profile you have to follow, like and comment on other accounts. I didn't have time to do that but I knew a few hashtags that I wanted to follow and the automation tool helped me tremendously.

When my goal was to grow my Facebook page, I invested $5/day for almost a year until I got the page up to 10,000. It paid off because I not only reached an audience that translated into sales, but it also gave me a level of credibility with the media and for speaking engagements my 10k+ followers are viewed as a platform.

Early on in my business, I took a short contract where I had to go in-house to create a social media plan for a government agency. It was a temporary assignment but it took over my schedule for three months and I couldn't allow my social media feed to lay dormant so I used an RSS to Twitter tool to automate my tweets for a period of time. It worked really well.

Your goal may be to get to your first 1000 or 2500 followers on Twitter. For the next three months I would engage on a weekly twitter chat to get my voice out there. I'd also write for larger sites and include my Twitter handle in my author bio to get my twitter account out there.

What is your social media goal?

Questions to consider

❖ What platform(s) will you focus on initially to help you build your personal brand?

❖ What media - short text/longform text/photo/video - makes the most sense for your skills and personal brand?

❖ What is one goal you have for social media that you can work on over the next three months?

❖ What tools will you use to make the work easier?

11
MAKE YOUR PITCH
PACKAGE YOUR IDEAS FOR THE MEDIA

As a former journalist, I will always have a soft spot for the media. Early Americans nicknamed it "the fourth estate" for a reason. But why is media important?

Media gives you **credibility** and positions you as the top choice. Like social proof, having media attention helps to show that you're a legitimate expert who has already been vetted. If you're selling services or products, it helps shorten the sales cycle. If you're selling yourself as a professional, having published national thought pieces or given media interviews gives puts you head and shoulders above other candidates.

Media also gives you **visibility** and helps you grow your audience beyond your personal network. One of the things that many people find frustrating about building a personal brand in the beginning is the idea of "marketing to strangers." You can't rely solely on the people who already know you to grow your visibility; you have to expand awareness of your skills and talents beyond your friends and family. That's one reason media is so important - it's a proven way to reach beyond your network and grow awareness of yourself more widely.

Myths keeping you from landing media

While you likely understand how media can help you, if you're like most everyday people, you may not believe that you can actually land media coverage for your personal brand. After speaking with thousands of people over the years, I've identified a few myths that may be holding you back.

Myth #1

You need a press release

As I shared in an article about social public relations for Mashable, the traditional press release is *dead*. Now I know that sounds extreme, so let me explain.

Traditionally, press releases were issued when big companies had important news to share about the business. That is still the case. Smaller companies and individuals may still need to issue a release to announce a company takeover, merger, a new product or a book launch.

However, for most of us press releases are not the way news will make it into the news cycle. For most of us, any media coverage we land we'll be due to direct outreach to a reporter, or to our story going "viral" and catching the attention of mainstream media through social media.

Myth #2
You have to have a publicist

As a communications professional who has worked as both a journalist and a publicist, I can assure you that this is not the case. In fact, many journalists prefer to hear from the expert, small business owner, inventor or advocate directly. They want to hear the "story" behind the pitch and make a connection with you.

Don't get me wrong: publicists are great. They can help you find and shape your story, and most of all, they have existing relationships with members of the media. But if you have a good handle on why what you're doing is newsworthy, and you carefully construct your pitch, don't feel that a publicist is a necessity to get coverage.

Myth #3
You're not ready yet

When it comes to getting media coverage, everyone can start somewhere.

Now, if you know you are camera shy and don't have a handle on your talking points, you may not be ready to do a live television interview. But could you do an e-mail or phone interview for a major blog? You may not be ready to go on live national radio for an hour, but could you share your story more informally on a podcast?

Myth #4
If they don't reach out, the media isn't interested

If you have reached out to a journalist with your

pitch and they haven't responded, you may think that because they haven't called you back, they don't want to interview you. Or if you don't hear back after one email or call, you may assume the media isn't interested.

Neither of these assumptions are necessarily true. As you may know, newsroom staffs have become increasingly burdened in recent years with fewer staff members expected to generate as much coverage as before. I always advise clients to pitch and follow up twice before moving on. Journalists are busy just like you, and sometimes they need reminders.

So don't be afraid to follow up.

Types of media opportunities

There are many types of media coverage opportunities for experts. Here's a rundown of the most common:

- local television news segments
- national television segments (the Holy Grail)
- local print newspapers (and their web sites)
- local and national magazines
- local radio
- national syndicated radio programs
- satellite radio
- industry newspapers and magazines
- high-traffic blogs and websites
- podcasts

Keep in mind, the same email pitch could generate a placement that could look many different ways. For example:

You could use the thought leadership content you brainstormed in chapter six and offer your own tips on a morning show expert segment. This would air on your region's local television news (Fox, ABC, CBS, or NBC in the United States) affiliate.

If you have a lifestyle business of some sort, you could offer health or fitness demonstrations for a lifestyle segment.

If you pitch a newspaper or magazine, your quote may be included in a larger story, or if there's breaking news on your topic of expertise you may be invited on a news panel with other experts.

The online environment has even more opportunities. A profile of you or recap of your tips on a business web site like Entrepreneur.com could open major doors.

For print newspapers, your story could look a few different ways as well. For example, you may be able share your thoughts as an expert article in the business, health or lifestyle section of the newspaper. Or the paper may want to write a profile of you as an executive to showcase a local success story.

If you own a business and have a compelling startup story, you want to share your "business story" in the local paper. Or you could even contribute an expert quote to the story a reporter is already working on.

Example placements

To give you an idea of how these stories may shape

up after your pitch, here are a few that I've placed.
- *When Being Yourself is Doing Too Much* - I shared this personal branding essay with wellness website Thrive Global for republication.
- *Make V-Day Stress-Free with these 5 Tips from Couples Counselors* - a marriage therapist was featured in this expert round-up story by Washington Post.
- *Small Business Advice: The five secrets to landing lucrative contracts with corporate clients* - a small business coach was asked to pen this guest story for the Washington Post small business section.
- *How We Made Six Figures On the Side* - the two owners of a catering company shared their story of earning significant income outside of their day jobs as a part of the Washington Business Journal's "How I Did It" series.

National media

While it isn't impossible, national press is much more difficult to get if you don't have previous traction in local press. I've had producers ask me to send them links to a client's reel before considering the expert for a national opportunity.

If you have your eye on a national segment like The Today Show or Good Morning America, your expertise will need to speak to a national issue or trend. You may want to create a reel of local television segments or footage of you speaking. You may also want to have a well-developed website (at the very least a well-optimized LinkedIn profile) that demonstrates your expertise. If you have a book, that's even better.

Find your newsworthiness

Throughout the year, there are times when your expertise will be more relevant than others. I call this finding your *media season*. For my work, the New Year is a great season because everyone is setting career, business, and life goals. This is also a great season for people in the fitness and health sectors.

Relationship experts are relevant in February around Valentine's Day. Financial experts are typically called upon in April as tax season looms. Career experts can gain traction in May with tips for new graduates. As a professional, while your season may not be as obvious, you can connect your expertise to a seasonal topic if you notice a trend in your work. What are some common issues that are coming up in your industry? Can you pitch a story based on that?

Industry and Trade Publications

Some professional fields have thriving industry publications, usually published by the membership associations that govern the industry.

For example, public relations professionals look to Public Relations Society of America (PRSA) and PRWeek to find the latest trends, case studies, and profiles of up and coming professionals. These industry publications are a great way to raise your profile within your industry.

In addition to featuring you in their publications, these industry associations and organizations are also a great place to start when looking for awards. Where can you apply or get nominated?

How to land coverage

If you're ready to take the next step of media visibility, first get clear on your expertise by identifying what you know. What is your core message? What are the top challenges people come to you with? What is your prescription for those challenges? Is the prescription universal? If so, you can offer expert advice on the topic.

Next, leverage the power of your story. Your expertise + a powerful story = *media magic*. Powerful personal stories move editors and producers to pick up the phone and call you in. Your story could be a personal triumph over tragedy, a personal transition, your status as the only or the first to do something extraordinary.

Then, determine your media relevance and find your seasonal hook. Look at national news and determine if you can localize a popular story. Or if there is a big story happening locally, can you tie it to a national trend? Or can you personally weigh in on a big news story that everyone is talking about?

For example, during a big federal government shut down, I was feverishly watching media coverage. After several days with no change in sight, I began to notice reporters were beginning to repeat themselves. But they couldn't shut down the story while so many thousands of workers were glued to their television screens and smartphones, waiting for word on when they could return to work.

I reached out to one particular reporter who was publishing daily on the shut down and pitched him about my clients - federal government employees who were using the time to beef up their web sites. I figured he could use a new story angle since he was publishing on the shut down daily. I was able to share a few names of clients he could interview, and he did.

I used the strategy to secure similar placements on a news talk radio station, Fox morning news and the LATimes. The pitch worked because it offered these reporters a new spin on a topic they were already covering. When a media topic has the world in its headlights, don't fight against the current of attention. What can you add to the conversation?

After you've decided on your media relevance, you'll need to identify your opportunities for coverage. Make a list of your top opportunities for local, national, broadcast, radio, magazines, blogs and newspapers. Who are the journalists who are covering your industry? What writers are covering your competitors? If you know your media relevance and have a list of journalists, you're finally ready to write your pitch.

Tips for writing a good pitch

First, you'll want to find a current phenomenon, compelling statistic or timely seasonal fact that positions the problem. For example, "Studies show that divorce filings peak in the month of March."

Then, you can introduce your solution or topic, yourself, and your expertise, i.e. "From my experience, couples who headed for divorce typically have had little to no communication for months. But there are four straightforward strategies they can use to improve communication and get their marriage back on track. As a marriage and family therapist, I've shared these strategies and helped dozens of couples reclaim connection."

Step three, and perhaps most importantly, ask for the interview. Let the producer or editor know you want the interview, and make your contact information crystal clear. "Would you like to have me on Great Day Omaha to share these strategies with your viewers? I can be reached at 555-123-4567 or by email at marriagetherapist@example.com"

Last, be sure to close with more information about yourself and business. Some may say this is your boilerplate information.

Reaching out to journalists

Once you've written your pitch, it's time to send it! Make sure to send the pitch to only one journalist at a time and customize the note you send. Think of your email pitch as any other email message you're sending to a friend. You wouldn't email every single person in an organization with the same request, so use common courtesy to approach an email with reporters the same way.

Because spam filters are so aggressive these days, I'd send the pitch email with no attachments. If you need to share a document, upload to your web site's files or to a file sharing service like Dropbox and link to where the file can be found.

If the journalist does respond, you also need to be extremely responsive. Reply as soon as humanly possible because they may move on to the next source if they don't hear from you in a timely fashion.

If you don't hear back from the journalist in three days or so, follow the email, phone, email follow-up rule. Call the news organization to try to make contact by phone, and if you don't reach anyone leave a voicemail and send an email about your voicemail. Then leave it alone.

There's a fine line between being appropriately aggressive and being a pest. Don't make the mistake of not following up at all. But also, don't send twenty emails to the same person. If they don't respond after a few attempts, they're most likely not interested.

Remember, if your first form of communication with a journalist is through email, it's your first impression with them. Don't think they won't remember your name if you're too pushy or rude.

Make time for media

Once you enter the media pitching stage of the process, you'll need to regularly set aside time for outreach. Landing media coverage is not a passive activity. Make sure you're doing all you can do to generate consistent coverage.

When I'm actively pitching a story, I set aside time each week to look for ideas, new contacts and reach out to reporters on my media list. I set up and check Google Alerts for mentions of my topic, keywords or competitors. I also make it a practice to look over the big news stories of the day just in case there is a national story I can take local or vice versa.

Finding journalists to pitch

There are many paid services that give you access to journalists' contact information. In the past, these databases have earned a reputation of being too pricey for individuals at several thousands of dollars per annual subscription. But these databases also encourage spam because they make it too easy to download contact information and blind copy journalists.

In the age of social media there are more crafty ways to secure contact details. You can find reporters on Twitter and start to engage with them by sharing their stories and commenting on what they're doing. You can - wait for it - *pick up the phone*. Most major news organizations have listed contact information on their web sites. Call directly and request to be connected.

You can also read publications and look for bylines, then try to connect with the people you've found on LinkedIn or through their personal web sties. If you look at a publication's masthead, many contact details can be found there or even at the end of a journalist's story.

Lastly, if you're more social, you can attend conferences and events to meet journalists in person.

After you land a media placement

Many people make the mistake of doing the hard

work to land a media placement, only to not fully leverage the coverage. Don't make that mistake! You can use media placements to build your brand in the days, months and years after securing the hit.

Leverage your media coverage

Don't let the placements happen and disappear. Promote your appearances on social media before the appearance, during the appearance and after the appearance.

If you have a television or satellite radio interview and the producers share the link afterwards, be sure to add that link to the media page on your web site. If you have a list of e-mail subscribers, send the story out to your list!

Remember, you can promote your placement more than once. It's not only relevant the day or week it airs or runs. You can "claim" old media placements on your LinkedIn profile, website and/or brochures forever!

Questions to consider

- ❖ What is your media worthy story?
- ❖ What are your most newsworthy times of year?
- ❖ Which part of your expertise could be packaged for a segment?
- ❖ What topic could you give a quote on?
- ❖ What publications exist for your industry?
- ❖ What television and radio programs would you be a good fit for?
- ❖ What journalists could be added to your media list?
- ❖ What is one tv or online media opportunity that you think you can can secure in the next month?
- ❖ What is one media opportunity you can secure in the next six months?

12
FIND YOUR STAGE
PACKAGE YOUR IDEAS FOR PUBLIC SPEAKING

Although public speaking consistently ranks as a top fear for most people, it also is one of the best ways to build your personal brand. But why is public speaking so important? From my experience, speaking helps build your brand in three distinct ways.

Scalability, visibility, authority

Speaking is typically the first way experts use to scale their time and talents. Even if you work full-time, you can quickly grow your audience by sharing your message to groups of people. Speaking leverages your time, and "scales your ideas" from one to one, to one to many.

Like media, speaking increases your visibility as it puts you in front of a much bigger audience than you'd have when having a one on one conversation.

Speaking also positions you as an authority. Regardless of what you're talking about, being the person in the front of the room signifies the power of your ideas.

Speaking has single-handedly changed my

business and established my position as an expert. It is hands down the fastest way to show your potential customers your expertise before you sell your expertise to them. It works much like the media but, when done right, creates a connection with the people in the audience.

Everyone can speak

No matter where you are in your business or in the growth of your personal brand, you're reading this book because you have some degree of expertise to share. You may not be ready to own the stage during your very own Ted Talk, but can you be a special guest for a webinar? Whether you're speaking on a panel at work or in the sanctuary at church, being on a stage of some sort creates an effect in the minds of those who make up your audience.

Your speaking engagement could look many different ways, for example:

- a panel with other experts
- a breakout session of a larger event
- a half-day bootcamp
- an office hours session during a conference
- a retreat presentation
- a conference keynote presentation
- a college commencement address
- a webinar
- an online conference or summit
- a twitter chat

Your message

Your speaking message is likely the same as your

core thought leadership message, but now you are packaging it for the stage. Depending on the type of speaking engagement you've been offered or what you're going after, your message could look a few different ways.

For example if you are speaking during an industry event, you may be asked to share a case study to showcase best practices for others in your industry. Or you may be asked to offer specific advice on an issue unique to your profession.

If you're asked to speak before an audience of young people at a university, or a faith-based audience at a church, you may share a personal story or career triumph. You'll likely be asked to connect your presentation to a larger theme.

A note on keynote presentations: while not impossible, paid keynote presentations are much more difficult to get if you don't have a previous brand platform, a strong reputation in your area, or a book. Depending on the cache of the event, you may have to send supporting documentation to vouch for your credibility the way you would for a national media interview. Here are some key questions to consider for each type of speaking opportunity:

Preparing for a keynote opportunity
- What is your personal story? What is your business or career story? With whom will this resonate?
- How did you take the road less traveled and still become a success?
- How have you triumphed and overcome major

obstacles?
- How do you inspire? Who do you inspire?
- How can you package your book, best podcast episode or best blog post, etc. into a stage-worthy message?

Panel Opportunities

- What are the potential questions? (While they may not send them, it's okay to request these).
- What are your talking points and main ideas about this topic?
- Where can you lend your voice to make a conversation richer?
- What perspective do you have that differs from that of the other people who typically show up? What hasn't been said before?

Breakout Opportunity

- What can you teach? What problem can you share a clear solution to?
- What tools, worksheets, or handouts can you share that might make it easier for the audience to navigate this solution?
- What is your formula or prescription? What are your 3-5 solid tactical pieces of advice to solve this specific problem?
- What are the clear take aways you can provide the audience?
- What questions can you ask or activities can you embed to make your presentation interactive?

Where to find speaking opportunities

There are many types of speaking opportunities

for experts. Depending on your experience, network and expertise, you may be eligible for paid or unpaid opportunities. Before you turn your nose up at unpaid opportunities and scoff at speaking for "exposure," take it from me: speaking for free can be a great way to build your personal brand! Especially for new speakers, it's a wonderful opportunity to practice your presentation and learn what resonates with your audience. Having done dozens of unpaid speaking engagements, I am grateful for the opportunity to get the kinks out of my talk. For many of my presentations, I learned as much about myself and my message as I shared!

Now don't get me wrong, speaking is hard work for which you should be paid. I now command 4-5 figures for bootcamp style speaking engagements that require me to distill my framework down into workshop style sessions. But I believe I earned the right to charge my fees over the years I put into to deepening my craft. If you're ready to add speaking as a revenue stream, here's a rundown of the most common paying opportunities:

Conferences and conventions

Annual conferences and conventions are a fantastic opportunity for you to share your message. Depending on the organizers, a good event may assemble hundreds or even thousands of people. The event marketing alone has the potential to expose your brand to thousands of new people. And in addition to registration or ticket sales, big conferences and conventions typically also have sponsors underwriting the event costs. Organizations that host annual conferences and conventions include professional associations, magazines and industry publications, national nonprofit organizations, women's organizations, constituent groups' organizations and other professional organizations.

Corporations

Sometimes, corporations will host their own industry events. For example, one year Guardian Life hosted an event called the Women Producer's Summit and I was hired to deliver the conference keynote. The event focused on women in the financial services, and Guardian brought me in because they wanted to inspire their female audience and help them with personal branding.

More recently, I've designed and delivered personal branding workshops for companies like AARP and Spotify. These companies brought me in to deliver a personal branding workshop for high potential students or participants in their fellowship and internship programs.

Colleges and Universities

One of my earliest paid keynote presentations was as a luncheon keynote for a Women's Day program at a small private university in South Carolina. I got a chance to tour the campus, meet with students and inspire them during a twenty minute keynote. It was so much fun!

Colleges and universities like that one typically

have seasonal programming where an external speaker is desired; they want someone who will resonate with their student body or graduating class. To find these types of opportunities, look at the event calendars for colleges and universities in your area. You can also check out past events to get a sense of the institution's event flow as well as they type of speakers they've hired in the past.

Churches

Many churches host retreats for different factions of their congregations. Sometimes they bring in non-religious speakers to speak at special services for Women's Day, Youth Day, etc. Does your church or another church in your area regularly invite speakers to share?

Could you be next?

Unpaid Speaking Opportunities

Small industry associations, local networking groups, student-led campus events, smaller church events and nonprofit groups that serve the community may not always be able to pay you to speak. However, they often have sizable networks that they will promote your talk to. This level of promotion is personal brand building gold!

Some of my best unpaid speaking experiences helped me earn thousands of dollars. At one retreat, I knew the audience was comprised of small business owners who needed help with marketing. My goal for the event was to sell copies of my home study toolkit The Branding Box. I delivered a presentation that set the box up as the "next step" and sold a nice number of units, making the unpaid talk worthwhile.

When I was still offering social public relations services to nonprofit organizations, I was invited to give a talk on social media at a conference geared towards cultural arts organizations. The attendees were all the heads of arts and culture organizations, and after a sold-out breakout session, I was able to sell six organizations on social media training and consulting services.

Worth it.

At yet another event, a well-known coach invited me to be the speaker at her event's VIP lunch. By positioning me as the luncheon speaker, she aligned me with her premium customers - the highest paying members of the audience. She also exposed me to her email list and set me up to sell my own coaching services to a targeted group of women who were ready to invest. I was able to walk away with several new clients from the luncheon.

Start where you are

If you've never spoken before, start where you are! Who might be willing to give you a microphone now so that you can get the practice you need to fine-tune your message? What message could you formalize?

For example, are you always giving crisis management advice to colleagues at work? Might they be willing to gather a group of 30 others from different departments within the company for a lunch and learn?

Are church members always asking you for productivity and home organizing advice? Could you assemble a group to hear you give a talk?

Is your networking organization or sorority made up of members of your target audience? Would they be receptive to you giving a presentation at a general body meeting?

The idea is to get into the game. By speaking in front of a group of people, you practice the art of sharing what you know. And when you take the experience further by sharing that you're speaking on your social media channels, that impact is compounded exponentially. Even the people who aren't there will be impressed that you were speaking somewhere.

Pitch yourself to speak

Landing speaking engagements is not as difficult as you might imagine. Many conferences and conventions hold what is known as a "Call for Speakers" or "Call for Presenters" where you'll have the opportunity to submit yourself. Obviously, as your brand grows, you'll begin to be approached for speaking opportunities. But in the beginning, you'll have to pitch yourself.

Even for unpaid opportunities there is still a pitch involved; you'll have to make yourself known to conference organizers or industry leaders. You can do this by attending their events and letting them know about your expertise.

At other times, you'll have to make yourself known. If you are the right expert at the right time with the right message, you'll just need that message to inform your pitch.

However, if you're going after a speaking opportunity that does not exist, i.e. you're trying to get brought in to teach or train, you will need to get a simple speaker's deck together that includes:
- your bio
- your photo
- your speaking topics
- your format availability
- your contact and booking information
- where you've spoken before
- any media or awards you've received

Questions to consider

❖ What topic can you deliver a solid 30-45 minute presentation on?

❖ What is one speaking engagement you can apply for?

❖ What is one conference, college, corporation or church that you've wanted to speak at or you've noticed and think you could offer your talents as a speaker?

❖ What speaking format would be easiest to try first?

13
WHO KNOWS YOU
BE INTENTIONAL ABOUT YOUR NETWORK

Serving as the featured public speaker is obviously the ideal way to attend events. But even if you're not speaking, you should still circulate at events to help grow both your network and your social media following. Attending events and networking helped me grow my online social media following and helped me create that *know, like and trust* factor when I was just starting out in communications in DC.

Power tip: even if you're not speaking and you are not on the program, you can still make yourself quite visible in two very distinct ways. First, you can take over an event's hashtag so that people can't help but notice you online. Do this by tweeting the thoughtful gems from the speakers (taking care to make them sound smart so they will retweet you) and sharing your own insights. Second, you can stand up and ask a question. If you're in a crowded room of 500 people and a panel just concluded, figure out a smart question you can ask the panel. This will give you an opportunity to introduce yourself and share what you do in front of a captive audience. Be careful to have a thoughtful question and not just a comment: no one likes a microphone hog who is only talking to promote themselves. But make sure that you preface your question with a polished introduction of yourself and if applicable, your business name.

Voila!

You just became visible to the entire room without being a speaker at the event.

Finding networking opportunities

If you're not sure how to find or narrow down your networking opportunities, ask yourself what audiences you want to reach and where those people tend to congregate. Think even further about what this audience needs now and what problem you can solve for them.

I'll cover more on how to go about finding places build your professional network in the chapter fourteen. But for now, keep this in mind: if you aren't strategic about where you circulate, you'll end up wasting a lot of time.

What voices surround you?

When it came time for me to declare a major in college, I remember telling my father that I planned to major in English. I didn't have a plan for what I would do with my English degree, but I knew that I loved to write. Even then, I was determined to pursue what energized me to see where it would lead.

I will never forget what my father said when I

proudly announced my planned major: English. My dad told me that if I majored in English, I'd end up as "the most well-spoken person working at McDonald's."

Ouch.

Those dismissive words hurt and shook my 18-year-old self confidence. What did I know about life, work, declaring majors or preparing for a career? My father was a successful engineer at the time. I valued his intellect and trusted his opinion. If he thought I was crazy to major in English, I must have been. But the thing is, I knew in my heart that he was wrong.

So I continued on my path to major in English. And I can tell you that I have not once regretted that decision. Staying true to myself allowed me the room to venture into journalism, creative writing, communications, and personal branding. A strong command of language has helped me communicate the power of my brand and many others, and characterize what is unique and special about brands and businesses.

I'm not sure exactly what made me ignore my father's words. I was so young! And who knew then how the internet would transform the global economy, how the way individuals find and are found for employment would shift, and how communications skills would be more valuable than ever? I don't fault my father for giving me the best perspective he had at the time, based on the working world he'd known. But his experience as a professional couldn't look less like what my experience has looked like.

I share this story because your network isn't just about the people who are in a position to help you ascend. Your network is made up of every single person who you come in contact with professionally and personally - each of those people impacts your success.

In my work, I interface daily with people who are on the cusp of change whether they're going from no brand to full personal brand platform, or from career underling to industry rockstar. One thing remains constant: if they don't have the most supportive voices around them, problems are bound to arise.

I get it. It's easy to cling to the people from the past when you're about to do something major because with all of the uncertainty brewing, you long for an anchor. With so much changing, you want to keep something familiar.

But holding onto an anchor can be dangerous. Everyone who is in your life today may get where you've been, but they may not fully understand where you're headed. And when people don't understand, they may unintentionally poison you with the negativity and nay-saying that comes from a lack of understanding.

When it comes time for you to finally step up and step out in a different way, when you finally muster up the courage to dream a bigger dream for yourself, if you don't have supportive, encouraging people in your circle, it may be better to keep your plans to yourself.

Keep quiet until you can find others who understand your vision and can support a new and more expansive version of you.

The power of a like-minded community

So many of us find ourselves with an unintentional, haphazard network of family members, coworkers and friends that we have had with us for the last several years, the last decade, or for our whole lives. And as we grow and evolve, the people in our lives may or may not be growing in the same direction.

When you've hit a certain level of success and yet are still hungry for more, the people around you may not understand it. And when the others around you can't understand you, it leaves you feeling alone. This is totally normal.

As you step out and stretch yourself and reach the next frontier that is your next level, make sure that you intentionally seek out like minds because it's so critical to have people in your corner who can cheer for you, validate you, and remind you why you have to keep climbing.

Unfortunately, many people abandon their goals and their dreams because they don't have people in their lives who are cheering them on. So if you don't have people in your life who are on the same page with you, find some people to create your own community of like minds. It's critical.

How to find like-minded colleagues

If you need a new community of like minds, take advantage of technology and look online. I regularly find new people, new thought leaders, new voices, new writers, and new podcasters on social media. Those are people that I may decide to reach out to to begin to cultivate a new relationship.

Even if you live in the middle of Kansas and no one in your town understands the things you're interested in, you can use the Internet to grow your network and find other like minds.

Once you find people, especially if they're not in your town or in your immediate geographic area, start attending events where you can meet the people who are passionate about the things that you're passionate about. And this will change as you change; the people who are on the path that you're on will shift as your path shifts. For example, after I started a podcast, I began looking for events for podcasters because podcasting was a new passion for me. The people in my professional circle who were not podcasting as well didn't understand my podcasting journey. By seeking out new people, I was fortunately able to develop new friendships solely based on my status as a podcaster.

Just because no one at your school or in your immediate network is interested in what you're interested in, don't be discouraged. You're not trapped in your geographic area. You can attend conferences where you can meet people in other places who have your interests and share your passions.

You can also use the Internet to find those communities and attend the events that are being organized by the leaders of those communities.

Another way to grow your network intentionally is to join networking or mastermind groups led by an influencer. When you identify a mentor or leader who is influential and has his or her own following, pay attention to the programming that they're putting out there. If you can find someone who's leading a community and you really agree with their philosophy, you like how they teach, you like their style, you like their personality and values, sign up for something they're doing.

Chances are, there will be other people who were attracted to that dynamic leader for similar reasons. More than likely, they have similar goals as you do. So sign up for their program, take an e-course, take an online course, join a mastermind. And if you've done all of those things and you are still feeling like you haven't found the community of like minds that really scratches your unique itch, then maybe it's time for you to create your own community.

Why not develop your own circle, your own event, your own twitter chat, where you can begin to create a community of your own? Then perhaps that twitter chat or online experience would grow into its own event experience that people from around the country and around the world could come to connect.

If you are looking for something that does not exist and you've looked around and you're sure that it does not exist in the format that you would like it to exist in, you don't have to wait for anything to host your own experience. Feel free to create it yourself. You have my permission.

Questions to Consider

- ❖ What is one networking event you can attend to meet your target audience?
- ❖ What is one industry award to apply or obtain a nomination for?
- ❖ Who in your life should you put some distance between while you're in the fragile stage of getting your brand off the ground?
- ❖ What relationships are already supportive? How can you nurture those relationships and be more intentional about the time you spend with those people?
- ❖ What events are happening in your local area where you can attend and grow your network?
- ❖ What events can you travel to?
- ❖ Which mentors or coaches do you follow and admire? What events or online communities do they host? How can you get involved?
- ❖ What event can you host?
- ❖ What offline or online community can you start?

STEP 5
SELL YOURSELF

I once had lunch with a friend who'd recently been laid off from a high profile job in media. She decided freelance PR was her next career step. She was of course nervous and afraid about starting out on her own, but at the same time she was excited - she'd always wanted to do her own thing.

I was personally thrilled for her - she has GREAT work experience and would be a no-brainer hire as a staffer or consultant. I was positive that as soon as she "put up her shingle," the offers would start rolling in.

About a month later we met up again in our same lunch spot. Her energy had changed from excitement to nervous anxiety. I could tell that she was worried and I asked her to tell me why.

Well, the offers hadn't come rolling in as she had expected. Freelance gigs had slowed to a trickle, and she was beginning to wonder if she could really make a go of it. At one point in our conversation, she even said she'd begun to consider looking for another full-time job.

I was flabbergasted - she had an AMAZING resume. She had great references and had even done work for celebrities. What had gone wrong?

As I began to probe her, the answer became clear. While indeed she wanted clients, she hadn't told anyone. She hadn't communicated her new availability to her network. She'd just expected the opportunities to find her. In fact, most people didn't even know that she was no longer at her full-time job.

For years, she'd worked in large organizations and promoted the work of her CEO. She was used to being behind the scenes - in the background so as not to outshine the higher ups. She'd never mastered the subtle art of promoting her own work.

"How do you expect people to know about you, if you don't tell them?" I asked. As she pondered her new reality, we began to formulate her plan.

She jotted down the action steps to really begin to show people WHAT she could do and WHY they should hire her. She made a list of people to call for meetings and created a script for how the conversation could flow. She began to realize that what had been missing all along was a strategy to sell herself to her network. With strategy in hand, she got excited. Bursting at the seams, she wanted to skip her afternoon meeting so she could go home right away and get to work.

When I checked in with her again just a week or so later, she'd made a complete 180. She had not only picked up 5 new clients, but now had others members of her network sending clients her way! She felt silly for having even contemplated looking for another job when her own marketing machine was right under her nose.

Another time, an old colleague of my husband contacted me after she was laid off. Formerly a director in a well-known national non-profit organization, she needed help rebranding herself to get a new job. She'd tried a little networking. She'd sent her resume out to a few leads, but at that point she wasn't getting any traction. After being in her position for over 8 years, her job-seeking skills were understandably rusty.

I asked her to tell me about her past experiences - what was she selling to people online and in the interview? As I probed, she began to tell me all of the cool things she'd done over the course of her career.

I was blown away!

But for some reason, when I looked over her resume and LinkedIn profile, they didn't quite match the accomplishments she was telling me about. I could quickly see that because she wasn't telling her full story, she was "leaving money on the table." By leaving out key information about some of her most important career wins, she wasn't letting potential hiring managers know exactly what she was capable of.

And like so many people I meet with, she wasn't selling herself. In fact, she was selling herself short. By being too modest, she wasn't claiming the full magnitude of her brilliance. She wasn't owning her leadership and strategic thinking skills. She wasn't taking credit for putting winning strategies in motion, or leading her team to victory.

Unfortunately, I see this all the time. So many high achievers (especially women) become desensitized to the amazing things they may have done 1, 3 or 5 years ago and forget how impressive their accomplishments are. Or, they take modesty too far, and fail to include the information that could potentially land them their next opportunity.

As for my husband's co-worker, we gave her resume

and LinkedIn profile a complete overhaul. Once we pulled out her true strengths, and articulated her past successes more accurately, even *she* was impressed. She'd actually forgotten about many of the notable things she'd done over the course of her career. In reading her new profile, it was as if she was meeting herself for the first time. She now could definitely see what she had to offer another organization.

And her new organization must have felt the same way, as she emailed me shortly thereafter to inform me that she landed another director position in her industry!

Can you relate? If you're looking for better opportunities - clients for your business or even a better paying job - you *have* to sell yourself. If you're not gaining traction in your career search, business, or opportunities for your personal brand ask yourself if you may be using the "no sales" approach like my friend, or the "undersell" approach like my husband's colleague. Whether you're either underselling yourself, or not selling yourself at all, its time to make a shift.

Ask yourself: what makes your experience, your skills, and your track record unique? Think back on the awards you've won, promotions received, and even pats on the back you've gotten. What prompted each of those individual moments of recognition?

Also, let's get real. Are you being too modest?

While they may seem mundane to you, your accomplishments are not. Otherwise everyone could brag about the same. Your past accomplishments have likely been extraordinary, and will be impressive to others - if you know how to frame them, and are willing to share them.

14
BE PROACTIVE
INTENTIONALLY DEVELOP OPPORTUNITIES

You may have heard the term "business development" used in the government contracting world. When I worked at a small public affairs firm shortly after college, I learned about the concept of creating a pipeline of new business partnerships and clients for the company. Even when we had client projects, our CEO was always working to market the firm, set up meetings, and court clients for the future. In those formative years of my life and career, I learned about the invaluable longterm mindset required to set your business up for the future.

That experience really helped me understand how opportunities worked. I watched our firm's founder finesse relationships over months - through in person meetings, phone calls, proposals. His patience was astounding, but required to land the type of six and seven figure deals that were the lifeblood of the company. One client meeting rarely led to a signed contract the next day. The best opportunities were the result of steadfast, dogged relationship building and expertise sharing over the course of months - sometimes even years.

Getting this birds-eye view early in my career undoubtedly shaped my long game approach to building a professional reputation and personal brand. I know it's not an overnight process.

In the same way you must set up a client-based business by courting new clients, submitting proposals and responding to requests for your capabilities, you must do that for your personal brand. If business development is consistently generating revenue by creating a pipeline of customers and clients, opportunity development then is the practice of consistently generating new opportunities for your personal brand. Both are a long game approach.

Opportunity development

Opportunity development is the act of creating new interest in yourself as a speaker, media commentator, expert and/or consultant. It's essentially working as your own public relations agent so you can grow and maintain relevance.

It's not enough to develop your thought leadership content and do the hard work of marketing yourself and your personal brand if you're not going to close the deal by making a pitch for your wonderful ideas, services, or yourself as an employee. This part of the book is meant to help you develop a strategy to identify new opportunities to sell yourself or what you have created.

In the previous chapters we discussed how you

can develop a breakout event, program or service both you and your clients will love. For some of you, that meant reconfiguring an existing offer or retooling an old presentation deck into a keynote speech. For others of you that meant creating something brand new. Either way, you still need to go about the business of securing opportunities for your expertise. Who might want to bring you on?

Look at past success

If you are already successfully pitching or selling to a segment, let's discover who your existing clients are. By taking a look at who you're already working with, you can pinpoint where you're getting the most traction, and figure out your strategic advantages.

Now before we go any further, let me clarify what I mean by "customers". I realize that not everyone is setting out to "sell" services or products direct to customer. You may be selling yourself for a promotion or new career opportunity outside your company, or even selling yourself as an expert for an unpaid speaking engagement or media segment to build your brand.

But even if money is not exchanged, you still need a strategy to sell yourself, which is what the following process details. If you struggle with the idea of a "customer," imagine an audience of people sitting in an auditorium listening to you deliver a keynote speech. Who's in the room?

Those are your customers.

You have an ideal audience

Who is naturally drawn to you? Where do they live? What are their demographic similarities? How do they think? What life, career or business stage are they typically in? Think about your customers geographically, demographically, and psychographically.

For example, do you typically help, attract, or resonate with:

- single professionals
- married couples
- mothers
- lawyers and attorneys
- businesswomen
- baby boomers
- millennial professionals
- single mothers
- divorced mothers
- pastors, bishops or other religious leaders

It's important to examine who is attracted to you because you may be unknowingly working with the *same type of person* over and over again. If that is the case for you, this is an opportunity to make your marketing reflect the people who *already* like you.

They're a much easier sell!

A small example: a few years ago I really began to show up authentically in my personal brand photography. Instead of my super tamed and straightened newscaster hairstyle, I'd settled on a set of natural corkscrew twists that framed my face beautifully. Shortly after I began to show up more authentically through my photos, I noticed that I was beginning to attract a lot of African-American women who also wore their hair naturally. On our discovery calls, these women would even reference my hair as something they liked. It resonated with them, and that created a sense of connection that made them want to do business with me.

I was surprised how such a small thing could attract people (and I'm sure it equally repelled others). But instead of ignoring the fact that so many of my clients were African-American women who wore natural hair, I began to double down on that aspect of both my identity and the imagery I used in my marketing materials.

On both social media and my website, I intentionally began to integrate stock photography that reflected beautiful women who wore natural hair. For me, this was a nod to my clients as well as a way to embrace my authentic self and connect with people who that resonates with as well.

Now, having a specific hairstyle is not a requirement to work with me, obviously. However at the time when many women had yet to embrace natural hair, it sent a strong visual message and helped create a sense of connection before I ever picked up the phone.

Around that same time, I also began to notice a disproportionate segment of my audience was comprised of recovering attorneys - women who had gone to school to become attorneys but were no longer happy in that profession. A common refrain that came up for many of my clients was that although they had pursued considerable training, they still were not fulfilled and were looking to find the work that made them feel more alive. That lack of fulfillment made them reach out to me. I began to integrate that message into my email newsletters, blog posts, and sales pages because I found that not only were educated women attracted to me, but I was much happier when working with people who fit that profile because I like to work with experts who are deeply entrenched in their subject matter.

Again, it is not a prerequisite to have advanced degrees to work with me, however it attracts a certain type of person when you start to speak their language.

So think about who you already attract. What are the similarities of the people who are always drawn to you? What are the similarities of the people who are always asking for your help, always asking for your advice, or always thanking you for the support you provide? Do they all live in the suburbs? Are they all parents? Are they all currently in graduate school?

Or perhaps the niche they occupy is situational: maybe they are about to get married, or they are pregnant with their first child, or they're about to embark on the first year of school for their first child. What personal milestone or life chapter have they reached that made them reach out to you?

Group strategy

Once you understand the mindset of the client, or the point of life that your favorite customers are in when they reach out to you, you can begin to market to them in the other places they naturally congregate.

For example, for a health coach who enjoys helping women get fit before their wedding day, it might make sense to pitch herself as a speaker to a wedding industry conference. Or it may make sense to sponsor a bridal show or some sort of wedding event where brides-to-be are attending to identify wedding vendors. It may also make sense to reach out to wedding planners to create a partnership.

Following up on my own example, a lot of the clients that I attract have earned doctorates and work as psychologists and therapists. It might make sense for me to attend a networking meeting for psychologists and therapists in my region if I wanted to specialize in working with that specific group.

A communications consultant who just launched her new business, may want to focus more on nonprofit professionals who need support with their communications and social media. In the Washington, DC area alone there are a number of networking groups and events for nonprofit professionals so that would be a perfect place for her to network and make her services known.

If you are a human resources consultant who helps business owners hire their first or second employee, going to small business networking receptions is obviously a smart strategy. If you see a conference that is focused on scaling and business growth, you can assume that audience is likely already thinking about these types of things.

The idea is to go where your most phenomenal potential clients are meeting en masse. You want to be at the conferences and events they are attending. You want to get your articles published in the magazines they're reading. You want to accept awards on stages and in front of audiences they respect. You want to apply to speak at conferences where this target market will be - not just conferences that are good for our visibility.

Individual strategy

While the macro strategy is very important and a much faster way to build your business and opportunity pipeline, another way to build the pipeline is to intentionally reach out to target client and set up meetings one on one.

We all have a list of dream clients we would love to work with. Michelle Obama is at the top of my list because I would love to help her think through her post-White House personal brand. But I also have a list of more accessible people I'd love the pleasure of working with as well.

I'm sure the same goes for you. You have your dream targets but you also have people in your existing network you've yet to tell about your work.

Get in front of your targets

It's not enough to merely write down your targets

- you must create a plan of action to get in front of them. Once you've made a list of targets, consider your approach. Who do you know within the organization or corporation you want to work with? Who is connected personally to the specific people you identified? Can that person potentially get you a meeting?

If you don't know someone who is directly connected to the person you want to reach, do you know someone who is connected by a third-degree who may be willing to introduce you to their connection? Get creative, and don't be afraid to use LinkedIn to see how your network is linked.

I love LinkedIn and have found it to be a great way to get to know new people who I may have never been able to meet out at a networking event. Getting involved on LinkedIn is fairly straight forward: start showing off your expertise by commenting on discussion threads. Send a connection request and note to someone whose comment you found interesting, and watch your connections grow.

But even if you are not on LinkedIn or don't use it regularly, you can still use a similar strategy to create a database of potential customers and strategically work your way down the list. Start with the networking events and conferences you will be attending in the next nine months. Who will be speaking, presenting and attending? Who do you want to meet once you get there, and how will you approach them?

Until you are in demand, get intentional about where you are spending your time, so you can meet the people who potentially fit your customer or audience profile.

Networking in your industry

It is worth mentioning that in the beginning, you will likely find value networking in your own industry. However, make sure you are networking in the places that your customers and audience members will be as well.

I learned this lesson the hard way.

When I first started networking after to grow my PR business, I networked very heavily in the communications space. I attended every industry event that I could afford to attend because I wanted to meet new people. I'm also a self-professed nerd and lifelong learner, so I was also hungry for the professional development. But after a while, I realized that I had amassed a very large network of other public relations professionals and communicators. I was absolutely able to leverage this network for a few other purposes - namely my signature events - however, few of those communications professionals ended up being clients until I started doing coaching work. I realized years into my ad hoc networking approach that I had expended a lot of energy to essentially grow a network of peers.

Now, don't get me wrong. I don't regret building my network that way. I made some wonderful friends and know smart people I can bounce PR ideas off of and collaborate with. However, if I were solely looking for people who would hire my business and I had to do it all over again, I would focus exclusively on organizations and associations focused on small business owners like the Chamber of Commerce or the National Association of Women Business Owners. I would have focused my efforts more broadly on networking groups that focused on business owners because those were the people who needed my services the most.

Set specific goals

You've probably never made specific, quantifiable goals about your personal brand but I encourage you to do so now. How many times do you want your advice featured in the media each quarter? How many views do you want to get on your LinkedIn profile each week? How many new clients do you want coming into your business this month?

If you have developed your signature offer and you have decided the price point for that offer, now it will be helpful to decide how many of those offers you would like to sell on an annual basis, a quarterly basis, a monthly basis, and a weekly basis. It helps to break it down so that you know if you are on track with your business development AND so you can set small goals that are easier to achieve.

For example, if I want to land four media interviews each month and out of each 10 journalists I talk to, one will typically bite, that means I need to talk to at least 40 members of the media each month in order to get in front of enough people to make my target. Think about yourself and how many people you realistically want to close.

Often times, people get excited and caught up when they see initial success, whether that is landing one media interview or making one sale. When you are building your brand on the side and you have a full-time income, one new opportunity may feel good to your ego, but for it to become a sustainable venture you will have to put structures in place to make those opportunities multiply on a consistent basis.

Have some numbers in mind for each month so that you know if you're getting close or if you're far away. Your numbers may be a monthly revenue target, or they may be a program target. But if you do not have a goal in mind, it will be impossible to reach. Think about your goal, verbalize it, and write it down.

Be intentional

It is important that you make opportunity development intentional. It's irresponsible to only think about landing speaking engagements when you're trying to build some buzz around yourself in the weeks before you interview for a new role. It's irresponsible to only think of adding clients to your pipeline when you realize you need more money, or you do not have anyone lined up for next month.

Opportunity development is an ongoing activity and an ongoing process. Remember, commit to the long game if you want your brand or business to grow.

For most people, it makes sense to dedicate at least one or two days each week to developing new leads. That does not necessarily mean that you have to spend the entire day reaching out to potential clients, conference organizers or journalists. But I do find that if you can allocate at least two hours twice a week for opportunity development, you should see success - especially if you are building this pipeline on the side of full-time employment.

In my personal experience, I dedicate Mondays to business development because I like to start the week with an idea of new clients I'll have the chance to potentially support. It's like a carrot that I dangle over the week that gives me a goal to reach. Will I be able to move this client closer to a close by the week's end?

Opportunity development process

Logistically, each week I block off several hours of my time for discovery sessions. I use an automated calendar and scheduling service to send out a link to people who have expressed an interest in working together. Once they reserve a time on my calendar, I set aside 15-30 minutes to get to know them, and share more about ways I could potentially support them through my products, services or group programs. But that phone call can't happen without a process by which I manage all of the incoming requests and correspondence from people who want to talk to me about their personal brand.

The idea of a process is important to note

because you likely have as much activity as the next person, but the reason you may not turned opportunities into a new role or paying clients is because you do not have a clear process around how you handle correspondence and incoming inquiries.

When people express interest in your work at a networking event, or reach out to you via social media and have questions about your expertise, that's the perfect opportunity to begin a conversation. What process will you put into place to ensure your hot lead doesn't cool?

Setting up the conversation

If you are at the stage in the conversation where the prospect wants to know more about you, having some sort of scheduling page or link on your website already setup is truly helpful because it eliminates the back-and-forth of trying to figure out a time when the two of you can meet, during which the interest can wane and the lead can go stale. So it's important to already have all of the things set up in anticipation of all the amazing clients who are going to be coming your way.

I recommend using the scheduling program as well as dedicating a page on your website for your contact information that begins the process. So a simple contact form or email address on your contact page will do.

If you are an employee, you don't necessarily have to use a scheduling service, but I'd recommend that you at least dedicate a window of time each week to take calls of this nature. Maybe it's only one hour each week divided into 30 minute slots. But whatever it is, plug it into your calendar and mark yourself as busy so others don't interrupt your opportunity development time.

Think ahead

We work so hard to land each opportunity, but often don't leverage the opportunities we have for more. If you land a media interview and the producer loves your take on a specific topic, propose a few other ideas for future segments in your follow-up email.

Or, if you are working with a client on an introductory set of problems, anticipate the next level of problems they may have. Is there a service that you currently have or can create to address the problems you can predict will arise?

For example, many people who work with me need an initial strategy as well as clarity around their personal brand. But once they have strategy and clarity, they need help with promotions. If they don't have a fully optimized Linkedin profile or web site, that is also a gap that I can help them fill. The initial problem is a lack of clarity and strategy, so I give them both. The next step if they don't have a web presence is I give them a home on the web. The third step might mean helping them promote the online presence and their expertise through public relations and media placements.

Think about the problems that could arise once

the initial problem you address is solved. And remember: you don't have to be the only person who solves every single challenge that arises. You can assemble a team that addresses each of the specific needs you see arise most frequently for your very best customers.

Ask for referrals

If you have clients, colleagues or members of the media who have had a great experience working with you, leverage those great experiences by asking for not only recommendations and testimonials, but referrals as well.

I have found that people are typically excited to refer you to someone they think you can help if they've had a great experience with you. While some people are very thoughtful and will refer you without prompting, many people don't think about it, so don't be afraid to request referrals from your existing clients. More often than not your clients will be thrilled to share your talents with the people they know and love.

Questions to consider

- ❖ List ten targets you'd like to work with.
- ❖ Identify a specific point of contact for each target.
- ❖ What audience is typically drawn to you?
- ❖ Where can you network to meet this audience en masse?
- ❖ Who can refer you to their network, and reflect on their great experience working with you?

15
MASTER YOUR TIME
TRAIN YOURSELF TO BE PRODUCTIVE

This is where the rubber hits the road. This is the chapter that separates the learners from the action-takers.

For it's not enough to know what to do; now it's about changing your thinking and making this a way of life. As you make personal branding a part of your life, it's going to be critical for you to encourage yourself and figure out what works for you moving forward.

Put Your Priorities on the Calendar

Alignment is everything. When I set out to get more serious about writing and publishing, I realized that although I fancied myself a writer, I wasn't making the time to write. My actual use of time wasn't aligned with my goals. There was no daily window on the calendar for writing. I hadn't created a routine; I wasn't sticking to a writing schedule. I didn't have a plan to actually reach my goals. But if writing books and publishing my ideas informed my identity as a writer, I realized I'd have to put writing on the calendar.

Once you establish a vision for your life or in this case your personal brand, you have to prioritize the actions that make that vision real.

Period.

Positive reinforcement

As we discussed in the previous chapter, the people around you can positively or negatively impact your productivity and state of mind. Get intentional and figure out who'll be in your support circle before you need them. Who in your life can serve to positively reinforce your brand building activities? Who in your immediate environment can serve as a cheerleader to help you keep focused and keep going?

Even if it's not someone who has also read the book, it's critical to find like minds that will cheer you on and will be able to understand what you're going through. You will want someone to bounce ideas off of and share resources with, and of course share your wins as you continue to land speaking engagements, media opportunities and interviews for clients or next level career roles.

Find your system and rhythm

I'm a big fan of task batching and task theming, a concept I first learned about in *The Four Hour Work Week* by Tim Ferris. Essentially, it's all about setting aside blocks of time to "batch" or "chunk" repetitive tasks. For example, instead of responding to email as it comes through out the day, you may set aside one hour during the day to reply to all of the email you received in a certain time period. Or, instead of sending out an email pitch every day, you may decide to set aside one afternoon each month to send out ten media pitches for the month.

You can be as detailed with this as you want but a schedule and rhythm that has worked for me for years even with young children, school pickups and after school activities is as follows:

On **Mondays** I work on business development and business administration tasks like sales calls, invoicing, proposals, etc.

On **Tuesdays** I focus on content. I spend time writing, working on blog posts, recording podcasts, writing social media content and my email newsletter.

I dedicate **Wednesdays** to backend client work, writing and media outreach for clients, brand strategy reports, and personal branding tasks like media outreach, speaking outreach or speaking engagement logistics. I also make time available for client sessions.

I reserve **Thursdays** for coaching sessions, strategy days and other client-centric meetings.

I reserve **Fridays** for a few hours of business development and follow up. Fridays are a half-day for me as my day ends at 1pm. Keep in mind, this is a schedule for an ideal week - sometimes the schedule changes. But it gives me a good starting point from which I can be flexible. It adds structure to my time and helps me set boundaries with everyone from myself to my family to my clients.

While this schedule works really well for me, I

encourage you to find what works best for *you*. If you work full-time at a corporate desk job, you have to intentionally find a time each week that is strictly for your brand if you want it to grow. I suggest dedicating one weeknight for opportunity development, and a weekend morning for content creation and scheduling

For example, if Tuesday nights are a night that are typically light for you, can you commit to business development from 8:00pm -9:30 pm? Then you could work on your content on Saturdays from 8:00 - 9:30 am. During that window you could write and schedule your Facebook posts for the week, respond to tweets, write and schedule your weekly blog post and newsletter, or record and episode of your podcast.

The point is you're going to have to make the time, which may mean sacrificing something. The good news is, the sacrifice may only be temporary.

Most successful personal brand initiatives require tremendous energy to get off the ground but are much easier to maintain once they've gained traction. Think of it as an investment: you'll be working hard to get your brand off the ground, but it will be much easier once you're further along in the process if you keep at it.

One thing at a time

Fight the urge to dabble. Be forewarned: as you begin to experiment and gain traction, you'll be tempted to start and market more than one project, more than one service, more than one speaking topic, more than one specialty, more than one signature.

Don't do it.

I can't impress upon you enough the importance of doing **one thing** successfully before moving on to the next. That means bringing one event to market successfully, or growing one social media platform, or mastering one signature talk. Trust me: in this process, tunnel vision will be your friend, for in the beginning, you don't have the luxury of fractured focus. Make some headway in one area and allow that headway to open the doors for you in others.

I did this with my signature offers, leveraging each to help me launch the next. I also did it with media - writing consistently for my blog before I pitched a national business magazine.

What is one thing you can focus on for the next three months? Put all of your energy and focus into that. Perhaps it's landing speaking engagements, maybe it's landing media placements, or growing your following on Twitter.

Get clear on your time

One thing that has been tremendously helpful to clients I've worked with is keeping a time log for at least one week so that you can see where your time goes. Similar to a food journal, a time log will allow you to see what is taking up your time, where you typically have extra time, where you're spending too much time and where you're not spending enough time.

For example, if after keeping a time journal for

one week you realize you're spending 4 hours each week on social media and only 15 minutes on business development and you have no clients, you know you need to allocate more time to business development and less to social media if your goal is to land more clients. So take an inventory of your days.

Batch your time

I have already a few ideas about task batching - the idea of taking a repetitive task and doing it over and over again instead of diverging your focus on several different tasks in that same window of time. For example, instead of writing and sending a media pitch, then writing the first part of a blog post, then writing a proposal for a new client all in the same one hour window (and doing none of them well), instead why not write and send four media pitches with that time? Or write a complete blog post, or customize your proposal template and send it to four potential clients?

Task theming takes batching to the next level by giving certain days or parts of a day a theme, i.e. business development Mondays in which the tasks I batch are discovery calls, proposal writing, etc. This is a little more difficult when you don't control your schedule, however it can be done.

Outsource, automate and delegate

If you can't make time for a certain aspect of your personal brand building, it may make sense to delegate it to someone who can do it faster and cheaper than you can. As you get busier, you'll realize that it isn't realistic for you to do it all. Social media management, for example, is something you can delegate to a professional who specializes in content.

But there are many other services and businesses you can use. You can use a virtual assistant to check your personal branding emails. To do this effectively, set up a special inbox just for your brand and give a virtual assistant access so he can respond to inquiries on your behalf.

Ideas for what to batch, theme and delegate
- emails
- social media management
- meetings and calls
- bookkeeping, invoicing and accounting
- business development
- customer service
- speaking outreach
- media outreach

Making time

Success with visibility and personal branding comes down to how disciplined and focused you're willing to be. It really becomes about finding and making the time to do the work.

Questions to consider

- Is your use of time in alignment with your goals?
- What tasks can you batch, theme and delegate?
- What's an ideal weekly personal branding schedule you can keep?
- What are some of the tasks that steal your productivity?
- Who can serve as an accountability partner or buddy to help you stay on track with your goals?

16
TELLING A TRUE STORY
UNDERSELLING YOURSELF, IMPOSTER SYNDROME

I have a friend who like me, works in communications. We actually met years ago when her company sponsored one of my early social media workshops.

If you were to ask her about what she does, she'd likely say something along the lines of *"I work in communications, like Amanda."*

But she and I - and the type of work we do - couldn't be more different.

She executes crisis communications programs from her global corporation's Washington office. And since I've known her, she's been the go-to person whenever a major communications crisis plagues the company. You've probably even seen her quoted in the NYTimes as a spokeswoman for one of the dozens of major crises she's navigated her employers through.

Crisis and I don't get along. I would *never* be able to do the kind of work she does and keep my stomach lining in tact. The stress would eat me up!

But to her? It's all in a day's work.

To begin telling the story that sells you, you must first get clear on how you do what you do better than others, so you can stop underselling yourself. And one of the biggest ways we undersell ourselves is through generalizations.

By oversimplifying her role and making it more general "I work in communications," you'd never know how dynamic and diplomatic this friend of mine is. Big companies that regularly face crisis issues may not know how valuable an asset she could be to their teams. If you met her you might make the mistake of asking her to write a press release, instead of asking her to advise you on how to bring the temperature down in a heated, publicly televised debate.

Which brings me back to you.

Are you regularly communicating what makes you different from the next person in your industry? Because if you want people to understand *and value* all that **you** bring to the table, you've got to let go of the generalizations and start talking specifics.

Generalizations don't explain the specific niche you occupy. Generalizations don't tell me how I can pay you to help me. Generalizations don't help me see how you're the best fit for a senior role at my company - the job you'd be perfect for, but aren't aware of yet. Generalizations don't make your value clear to people who haven't worked directly with you and aren't familiar with your work. And when they aren't clear about what you do, they're less likely to refer you to others.

How are you currently talking about your role, position and value? Is your description one generalization after another? Or is it specific, magnetic and captivating?

When you describe yourself in person at networking events or during job interviews, are you highlighting the most compelling aspect of your background?

Or are you burying the lede?

There's one particular block that shows up time and time again for my clients. Despite their incredible resumes, work ethics, and work histories the high achieving clients who are most drawn to me are all underselling themselves. And it has everything to do with the high standards that have made them so high achieving in the first place.

Don't get me wrong, high standards are great. But placed within the context of self-promotion, high standards coupled with a high achieving mindset create a cruel irony.

Because the high achiever is relentlessly raising the bar, they constantly judge themselves and diminish their own achievements against an impossible standard. Diminished achievements are seldom spoken of in company meetings, in job interviews or at networking receptions with potential new clients. Diminished achievements rarely make it into the bio, resume or Linkedin profile where they could help tell the world what that person is really capable of.

If you too are a high achiever and are looking to break through to your next level, consider just a few of the ways you may be diminishing your achievements, undervaluing your talents and underselling yourself.

Stop conflating your compensation with your professional value.

In our income obsessed society, this is easy to do.

However, despite their contributions to their company's bottom line, many employees are grossly underpaid. If that resonates with you, beware of making assumptions about your value, worth and income potential based solely on the figure that currently appears on your paycheck. You likely have the potential to earn much more.

If you're already working with clients and don't feel you're being paid what you're worth, it may be time to talk with a business coach or do some research on what others who are performing similar duties are being paid. When you are more educated on the norms of your industry, you can negotiate from a place of power.

Own all the value

You're likely not claiming and communicating all of the value you add.

I see this a lot when people find themselves adding value outside of their formal job description or scope of client work.

For example, you may be hired to manage budgets but you consistently bring your team leadership and project management skills to the table. If you regularly find yourself adding value for which you have not been hired or explicitly directed (and paid) to do, that doesn't negate the value of the work you provide. You have the right to claim work that falls outside of your job description when you're selling yourself in job interviews or client meetings. Figure out how this work helps to tell your full story and weave it into your narrative.

Sidebar - by learning to communicate ALL that you add in your current role or with your current clients, you can position yourself for a raise or new opportunity elsewhere.

Take the credit

You're likely not taking credit for your contribution to team efforts.

This is a BIG one.

For some reason, high achievers don't like to "take credit" unless they can say a project was theirs from start to finish.

But when working with large teams, everyone plays a part.

You don't have to claim full credit for team results, but you also don't have to understate your contribution, either. Maybe you played a part in that presentation by doing the research on the backend, and gathering all of the relevant case studies. Or maybe your contribution was "softer" - you kept the team organized, motivated and moving. Or better still, maybe you came in much later in the project but were able to get everyone refocused and energized after months of stagnation. Whatever role you played in the team dynamic, own it.

Downplaying your accomplishments

If you're like most naturally modest people I know, you regularly downplay former wins. This is the gaffe I see the most, and as a high achiever I understand where it comes from. Many of us think that we're only as good as our last project or role, when in actuality one role can't accurately define your personal brand. One project can't possibly tell your full story.

While your personal brand should absolutely reflect your most current wins, don't be so quick to dismiss big projects you worked on in the past. If you've switched industries or made a huge pivot, make sure you're weaving your past into your current narrative if it adds value.

For example, while I haven't worked as a full-time journalist in quite some time, the training I received working in a newsroom is a big part of how I'm able to help clients get clear on their brand stories. So I make sure to include that in my bio and whenever I'm selling myself in a new scenario.

If you're working with clients, don't downplay the value you added to projects last year and the year before. **It all matters.** And it's all valuable information that can tell your story and communicate how you are the right fit for the opportunity that's on the table.

Get in the habit of keeping track of your wins and creating language that describes what you've done in each project and role so you're not scrambling to remember your contribution, and you're not relying on only your most recent work to sell yourself.

Hiding the remarkable parts

Do you downplay what's most remarkable? This one is easy to do. You're close to your genius so you likely don't see it as such. (Tip: ask someone close to you if you're guilty of this one).

The thing is, most of us **grossly underestimate** the value of our most remarkable assets. We can come up with taglines and slogans in the shower - but no one would pay for that, right? We can walk into a heated discussion and immediately cool things down with our skills of diplomacy and conflict resolution - but everyone can do that, right?

Wrong.

Understanding your "genius" or what is most remarkable about how you're able to do what you do (typically faster than others, with more ease than others, or in a much bigger way than others can do given the same constraints) requires tremendous introspection.

Because most of us have a blindspot when it comes to our gifts, here an outside voice may be helpful. Talk to trusted colleagues, advisors, mentors or seek out a coach who is skilled in this area.

The bottom line is this: if you want to tell a story that sells you into new and better opportunities, you owe it to yourself to own all of your value. You owe it to yourself to claim everything you bring to the table.

Questions to Consider

- ❖ Where are you being too modest in your personal brand?
- ❖ What remarkable parts of your work could you be downplaying?
- ❖ What major accomplishments or career wins do you fail to bring up in conversation?
- ❖ When was the last time you made a list of your accomplishments?
- ❖ Are you intentionally hiding past accomplishments or team accomplishments for fear that they don't "count"?

AFTERWORD

THE MINDSET FOR SUCCESS

Some time ago, I was in the launch phase of one of my personal branding programs when I saw two other programs launching at the same time. The other programs covered a similar topic as mine, were at a comparable price point and targeted what I thought was a similar audience.

I shared those programs with one of my company's advisors to get her thoughts.

Honestly, I think I was looking for her to confirm my own insecurities and tell me that since all of these competitive programs were launching at the same time, I should wait to launch mine.

She looked over the information for both programs and agreed they both were compelling. However to my surprise, she expressed that she'd never invest in either.

Why? Because she didn't know either teacher. She didn't trust them.

She trusted me.

Trust as a competitive advantage

I went on to successfully launch that program and fill it with a group of students who knew my work and trusted my expertise despite the programs of my competitors.

I realized that even if others have similar offers, my brand resonates with the people who know and trust *me*.

The same goes for you. The point of doing the work to build your brand is to build the most important asset: trust. If your audience and network trusts you versus the other voices that are speaking on your topic, that trust is your competitive advantage.

You may think your industry of expertise is overcrowded. You may wonder what difference your contribution will make. Will it even resonate or have the power to break through?

I firmly believe **you** have a unique message that will resonate with YOUR audience - even if there are other people in your industry who are seemingly doing or saying the same thing.

Don't worry about what others are saying or offering.

Don't worry if what you want to say has been said before.

Don't worry that the space is overcrowded.

If you have a message and have encountered people who need to know what you have to teach, share what you know.

I guarantee that it will resonate with the people it's meant to resonate with.

Your work matters.

Inner work vs. outer work

When most people think about personal branding, they consider of the fun splashy side - the outer marketing of oneself through speaking, social media and landing press.

But there's another component - an arguably less glamorous one - that we don't often think about. It's the tremendous **inner courage** required for you to step up and claim your dream.

When it's time to enter into a new season of visibility, expect every feeling that's kept you out of the limelight in the past to surface.

When things don't go perfectly or according to plan, your default forms of resistance will push you back into old patterns.

You'll notice that you suddenly become **too busy** and don't have the time to commit to your goals. *Resistance*.

Or you'll be **unreasonably** hard on yourself. You may become **paralyzed by your need for things to be perfect** before anyone can judge your effort. *Resistance*.

You may second guess your ideas, reflect on past failures and give up before you even get started. *Resistance*.

Fear, self doubt and memories of past failure are often just enough to cripple most people and prevent them from putting themselves out there. But quiet as kept, it's all a part of the personal branding process.

The secret is this: people who achieve the most success are somehow able to push past the discomfort of failure and overcome the tyranny of self doubt. They go for it anyway.

These individuals are internally fortified - they embrace both the outer work and the inner work of personal branding.

If you don't have time to start an organization or passion project, but you could use an extra dose of confidence in your life, here are five simple ways to activate your confidence on a daily basis.

Review your accomplishments

Whenever I need a quick jolt of confidence before a speaking engagement, media interview or important meeting, I remind myself why I've been invited to the room. I remind myself that I have a seat at this particular table because I have earned it.

When applicable, I will think of a recent win or accomplishment in this particular area and remember how good it felt to succeed, how effortlessly I was able to accomplish my goals, and how I have everything within me necessary to do it all again.

Confidence then becomes a function of memory – if you lack confidence around a new opportunity, remember why you got the opportunity in the first place.

Take one step

Most of us have a big project or goal that has been hanging over our heads for months, sometimes even years. But by taking one small step in the direction of that goal, or doing one small thing in preparation for the project, we can begin to remove our mental barriers around it and activate our confidence.

For example, you may have always dreamed of writing a book, but the idea of writing a book is a daunting task. Instead of beating yourself up over not having done anything despite having had this as a goal for years, challenge yourself to take one step and work on an outline. Once you have an outline of your proposed chapters, challenge yourself to take a step by writing one page. With each step you take, you increase your momentum, and momentum is the ultimate confidence booster. Resist the urge to think you have to do it all in one sitting, or at one time. The journey of a thousand miles begins with a single step.

Do your best to look the part

It's hard to not feel confident when you're in a beautiful space or wearing a beautiful outfit. So until you feel confidence, try your best to look the part, because as the adage goes, when you look good you feel good!

When your confidence is down, sprucing up your space and appearance really helps because it shifts your energy and disrupts the message that you are unworthy of whatever opportunities have come your way.

Clean up your messy desk and make it a welcoming space to work. Invigorate your space with fresh flowers. Wear your new shade of lipstick, or put on your favorite dress. Surround yourself with items that make you feel good and eventually your attitude will have no choice but to catch up!

Veer away from your routine

A big part of confidence is knowing that you can tackle unknown challenges. But when we don't feel confident, we lack the moxie to get out there and do new things. By getting out of your routine, you flex your exploration muscles and show yourself that you can operate in new spaces or places successfully.

So many of us are living day to day on autopilot. Get out of your routine by taking a new route to work, trying a new restaurant at lunch, or striking up a conversation with someone new. You'll find the simple change will wake you up and take your brain off autopilot.

Mix the awakened brain with successful navigation of a new circumstance or surrounding and the result is increased confidence.

And when you shake things up and surprise yourself, even in a small way, you get a chance to see how limitless you are.

Questions to Consider

- ❖ Where could you stand to have a bit more confidence?
- ❖ What steps will you take to incrementally build your confidence in this area?
- ❖ How is comparison robbing you of the satisfaction you deserve?
- ❖ Is imposter syndrome an issue for you?
- ❖ What self-defeating negative messages do you need to confront in order to make yourself more visible?

NOTES

NOTES

RECOMMENDED READING

- **Michael Bungay Stanier** *Do More Great Work*
- **Marcus Buckingham** - *Now Discover Your Strengths, Go Put Your Strengths to Work*
- **Tom Rath** - *Strengthsfinder 2.0*
- **Tara Mohr** - *Playing Big: Find Your Voice, Your Mission, Your Message*

RECOMMENDED RESOURCES

The Branding Box - If you're looking for a deeper dive, check out the personal branding home study system at thebrandingbox.com. As your gift from the author, use the code **lastpage** for a significant discount!

Learn more about Amanda, The Branding Box and the Package Your Genius Academy

packageyourgenius.co
amandamillerlittlejohn.com
packageyourgeniusacademy.com
thebrandingbox.com

ABOUT THE AUTHOR

AMANDA MILLER LITTLEJOHN is an idea oven, brand problem solver, and creative powerhouse working at the intersection of public relations, journalism, marketing and social media. A former full-time print journalist and a writer first by training and passion, Amanda uses her unique storytelling lens and new media skills to help her clients uncover and subsequently share better brand stories.

A passionate teacher and trainer, Amanda is a motivating business coach for budding entrepreneurs and experts who are seeking brand clarity, new marketing perspectives, or fresh ideas on how to emerge as experts in their chosen fields. She helps people uncover their "unique genius" in order to share it with the world.

High achievers across the globe - from San Francisco to Saudi Arabia trust Amanda as their coach. Her clients have spanned industries - from government appointees to non profit leaders to academic researchers to CEOs. She has coached senior leaders from corporations including Spotify, Intel, JP Morgan, Scholastic, COTY/Cover Girl, Colgate-Palmolive, EY, WalMart, Guardian Life, Google, TD Bank and Johnson & Johnson.

Amanda lives with her husband Marc and two sons in Washington, DC.

Made in United States
Orlando, FL
03 May 2025